Growing Plants from Seed

Growing Plants from Seed

Richard Gorer

With drawings by Peter Barefoot

FABER AND FABER
London & Boston

First published in 1978
by Faber and Faber Limited
3 Queen Square London WC1N 3AU
Printed in Great Britain by
Latimer Trend & Company Ltd Plymouth
All rights reserved

British Library Cataloguing in Publication Data

Gorer, Richard
Growing plants from seed.
1. Flower gardening   2. Seeds
I. Title
635.9′42   SB406

ISBN 0–571–11148–3
ISBN 0–571–11149–1   Pbk

Contents

Contents

Illustrations

In this book metric scale measurements and British standard equivalents are given side by side. In order to give a figure of practical use to the gardener the equivalents shown are sometimes approximate.

Introduction

Since the critics have always been extremely kind to my writings, perhaps I can return the compliment and save them some trouble by pointing out that this little book tends to fall between two stools. Part of it is somewhat elementary and is designed for those gardeners who are starting to raise plants from seed for the first time, while other parts will be of more use to the more experienced gardener. The explanation is simple enough. Most writings on seeds and germination are scattered in various papers in various journals and this volume is rather a compilation of these papers than an original work. It is not easy to find all the scattered references and it is by no means improbable that I may have missed some; but I trust that at least the majority have been summarized in the following pages, which will thus constitute the first complete volume in which the various facts can be found gathered together. The work of P. A. Thompson in this field is particularly valuable and no doubt he will eventually produce a much more comprehensive volume than mine.

In the meantime I hope that this work will prove timely. Economics are forcing many people to attempt plants from seed, where previously they could have afforded plants, and the experience may be new to them. Personally I would always rather grow plants from seed if the waiting time were not inordinately long. I know few experiences to equal the excitement of seeing an unknown plant coming into flower for the first time.

I would particularly like to thank Mr. Alan Bloom of Bressingham Gardens, Diss, Norfolk, who must know more about raising herbaceous plants from seed than most of us, for giving me much valuable information.

1 On seeds in general

With the price of plants rising in common with the upward trend for everything else, it is obviously rewarding to raise your own, rather than buy from the nursery. Also, one of the easiest ways of growing plants is to raise them from seed, though, as we shall see, this is not possible in all cases.

Plants that botanists call cultivars and that others call named varieties can usually only be propagated by asexual methods; cuttings, layers or division. In the same category come F_1 hybrids, which are raised from seed, but from a seed produced by pollinating a particular mother plant with pollen from a particular father plant. This has to be done each time the F_1 seed is produced. Although this F_1 plant may produce seed, the plants so raised will neither be uniform with each other as is the case in the parent generation nor will they necessarily be as floriferous or as fruitful as their parents and it may well prove a waste of time to raise a second generation of an F_1 plant. This is not necessarily true for ordinary hybrid plants, but we shall be looking at those in more detail in Chapter 8.

With these exceptions there are no plants that cannot be raised from seed, but, as we shall see, this is not necessarily a straightforward process. Though with the majority of seeds it is just a question of preparing an appropriate seed compost, sowing the seed, giving it warmth, moisture and air and germination follows, it is not always as simple as that. For example, most plants of temperate climes like to germinate in the spring and so many seeds have an inbuilt germination inhibitor, which is destroyed by frost. This means that the seed, for example, of a crocus will be shed in May or June, but will lie in the soil until they have been frozen; then, as soon as it becomes warm enough, they germinate. There are a number of seeds that require this cold treatment before they will germinate. Fortunately, this is always available naturally, although it can also be supplied artificially, so this is not a problem when getting such seeds to germinate. A rather different case is that of seeds that are normally eaten by birds or other animals. Passing through the stomachs and intestines of such animals removes a germination inhibitor and once they have passed through the animals, the seeds usually germinate readily; it is when they have not been eaten that germination becomes difficult. In Argentina there is an edible passion fruit that is frequently planted for a crop, but seed if collected from the fruits in the ordinary way germinates very badly. What the gardener has to do is to eat a fruit and the next day defecate on his seed bed, when the seeds will germinate extremely well and rapidly. Fortunately such extreme cases are rare. There is a wild tomato on the Galapagos, which has become even more specialized; the seed will only germinate after it has passed through the giant tortoise; it seems that there is no germination if any other animal has eaten the fruit. We are most likely to meet this phenomenon with the seeds of hawthorns. Seed that has passed through a bird will germinate in the spring, but if we collect the haws and sow them, a wait of eighteen months is usually necessary, before germination starts. Space is saved by a technique known as stratification, which we shall be considering shortly.

You may be wondering why some seeds behave in this extraordinary way. Nature does nothing without a reason and it is usually a case of finding out what the reasons are. In the case of fruits and their seeds the reason is dispersal. Plants cannot move and in the case of long-lived woody subjects there is little chance for the seedlings to survive in the shade of their parents, so there is little point in seeds that have fallen from the tree germinating. Once the fruit has been eaten by a bird the seeds will be dropped at some distance away from the parent tree and one may hope that at least some will fall in a desirable position where they can thrive and make a fresh tree. Nature, of course, is extraordinarily wasteful. Most of the fruits from any tree will come to nothing. This is satisfactory in nature where balance reigns, but it is not what the gardener requires. He wants his seeds to germinate well and most to do so at the same time, and ensuring this is one of his tasks.

Let us consider the question of dispersal a little further. As we have seen one way of ensuring this is to surround the seed with some palatable pulp, so that the seeds are eaten and later voided. A less satisfactory way would seem to be for the seed itself to be edible. As we know squirrels will eat hazel nuts. Fortunately they also bury some for eating later and frequently forget where they have interred them; and possibly some die after burying the nuts. Birds like jays also pick up nuts, such as acorns and these are sometimes dropped before being eaten. It all sounds very haphazard, but it works.

The birds and other animals that eat fruits and nuts at least get something out of it, but other seeds, such as burdock and cleavers, attach themselves to the fur of animals brushing against them and get distributed in this way. It is a fairly successful method, but it is only possible for seeds that are carried fairly near the ground and in districts where there are sufficient fur-bearing animals. It is not a method of distribution that trees would find effective. Insects are sometimes called into play. Cyclamen deposit their seeds on top of their corms, but the seeds are coated with a sweet substance which attracts ants, who carry the seed away to remove this elaiosome, as it is called.

Easily the most popular seed disperser is the wind and plants have evolved numerous methods to take advantage of it. Tall plants are liable to have winged fruits, known as samaras, so that the seeds can skim away some distance from their parents. Such seeds as the ash keys and the propellor-like seeds of maples and sycamores are well-known, but there are many similar devices employed by plants the world over. Other plants, such as groundsel, dandelions, rosebay willowherb and many others equip their seeds with little balloons or parachutes, which enable

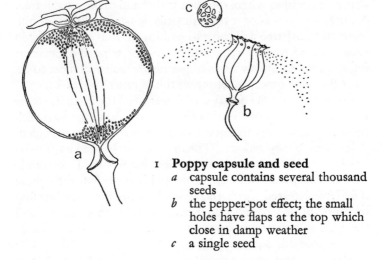

1 **Poppy capsule and seed**
   a capsule contains several thousand
        seeds
   b the pepper-pot effect; the small
        holes have flaps at the top which
        close in damp weather
   c a single seed

the seeds to float, on occasion, many miles. If the seeds are very
small no especial device is necessary, but care must be taken
that the seed is only released when a wind is blowing. A plant
like the poppy has a seed capsule rather like a pepper-pot and
when this is shaken by the wind the seeds are thrown out. Even
if they do not travel very far from the parent plant at first, they
can be blown further along the ground by subsequent winds
and can eventually be transported a considerable distance. The
colonization of bombed sites by the buddleia, the Oxford ragwort and the rosebay willow herb must surely have been due
almost entirely to wind dispersal. This is easy enough to understand in the case of the groundsel and willow herb which with
their silken parachutes can travel considerable distance in the
wind, but with the buddleia it is not so clear. Admittedly it has
a very small seed, which might be expected to be wind-borne
for some distance, but it may well be birds which are the real
transporting agents. Buddleia seeds may be distributed widely
over Great Britain, although in normal vegetation the young
plants are smothered when very small, but in bombed sites and
similar situations that are not conducive to the growth of most

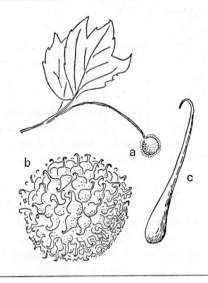

a seed capsule
b capsule showing
   hooks at various
   angles
c an individual hook

d a plant with seeds
e a seed cluster
f each seed is
   attached to its
   individual cluster

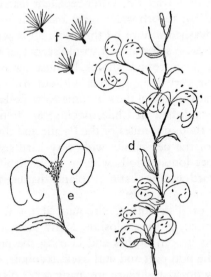

2 **Seed distribution** *above*: Plane; *below*: Willow herb

native plants, they are able to establish themselves without over-much competition. We know that this applies to the Oxford ragwort, which spread originally from the Oxford Botanic Garden along the clinker embankments of the railway, and the willow herb is also known as fireweed, for its ability to colonize burnt areas before other plants can recolonize them.

Some plants are even more enterprising. The erodiums, the stork's bills, not only have a silken plume to distribute the seed on the wind, but when the seed eventually drops, the plume, in moist weather, curls like a screw and plants the seed firmly in the soil.

Some seeds can be dispersed by water and, as one might expect, normally these are plants of the streamside and of the coast. As a general rule seeds are heavier than water and soon sink if they are moistened, but seeds that rely on water for their dispersal not only have air sacs which keep them floating, but are also covered with some compound which will prevent them becoming wet. After a time this water-repellent material disappears and the seed can absorb water again and germinate; provided it has been washed ashore by this time all is well. Some seeds can even tolerate salt water. It would seem that the coconut is so widespread on tropical shores, because the nuts can float in the sea for very long periods without damage. Smaller seeds also take advantage of the sea; some New Zealand hebes have become established in Chile, having, apparently, floated across so many thousand miles of the Pacific and there are various members of the pea family with very hard seeds which can float for very long periods without their viability being impaired. It is worth noting that most plants that use the sea for dispersal dwell in the tropics.

A popular method of distribution, although it must, of necessity be rather limited, is by explosion. Many of us can remember walking past broom bushes and hearing the pods crack, as the sides of the pod part and curl back in spirals, expelling the seed as they do so and there are many other plants which employ similar techniques. Visitors to the Mediterranean may have seen the squirting cucumber, which, when ripe, ex-

pels its seeds in a stream of gluey substance, which may trans-
port the plants up to seven meters. Balsam (impatiens) seeds
are very hard to gather as the capsules unroll at a touch, pro-
jecting the seeds some distance from the plant. In the case of
the policeman's helmet (*I. roylei*) once this seed has been ejected
it can be carried further by water, with the result that many
British streams are now lined with this Himalayan plant.

This need for dispersal is one reason why seeds differ so much
in size. On the one hand we have such minute seeds as those of
begonias and orchids, which can travel vast distances in the wind.
It would seem that the arrival of the North American ladies'
tresses (*Spiranthes romanzoffiana*) in western Eire at the end of
the eighteenth century and its subsequent spread to Scotland
and Devonshire, is entirely due to wind-blown seeds. On the
other hand you have really massive seeds like the coconut and
the monster coco-de-mer with a seed that may weigh 27 kg
(60 lb) and is 46 cm (18 in) long. Unless you can use the tides,
as the coconut does, it is very difficult for large seeds to be
widely distributed. The coco-de-mer has never been able to
move away from the Seychelles, where it is mainly confined to
a single population. On the other hand when a large seed
germinates it has a better chance of survival, as the large seed
contains ample seed reserves and, in some cases, such as the
coconut, water reserves as well. Very minute seeds have practically no reserves at all, so that even a few days' drought after
germination can result in the death of the seedling.

Some small-seeded plants, such as the orchids and many of the
heath family have to be invaded by a fungus before they develop
and the two plants live symbiotically together; the fungus providing nourishment in the early stages and also obtaining
nourishment from the developing plant. Usually the plant ends
by absorbing the fungus completely, so it is not altogether an
ideal relationship. Most green plants seem to have some sort of
a relationship with fungi, but it does not always assume the
importance in the early stages that it certainly has in the case of
orchids and probably with other families.

Although plants from small seeds have some difficulty in

surviving in the first few months, there is the advantage that enormous numbers of seeds can be produced with comparatively small outlay of energy and, as we have seen, these seeds are liable to be distributed over a wide area, so that the chances of survival and increase are considerably enhanced, even though at appalling cost in seeds that may never even germinate, let alone arrive at a seed-bearing stage themselves.

Leaving aside such anomalies as the coconut, one would expect that large seeds would be useful for rather slow-growing, long-lived plants. The acorn is a typical example. The tree grows slowly and for its first year or so its young leaves are liable to be overshadowed by weeds and grasses. If green-leaved plants cannot get to the light they will probably die, but the large reserves in the acorn will generally see that the young plants survive their first two years. If you grow an acorn in a pot and look at it after a year, you will still see plenty of reserve in the original acorn. This seems a neat logical explanation, but it will not stand up to much examination. After all, the broad bean is nearly as large as the acorn, yet here we are dealing with a rapid-growing annual plant, which one would not expect to need much in the way of food reserves, while on the other hand the eucalyptus, which include some of the largest trees known, have very minute seeds, yet they are probably the most successful Australian trees. Admittedly they are not slow-growing like oaks, but even so for the first few weeks they must be at a great disadvantage. Here again it is probably the weight of numbers which explains their success, but there seems no single reason why some plants should have small seeds, while others have large ones.

When we sow seeds we expect that after a suitable period the majority will germinate and with plants that have been cultivated in gardens for some time this is usually what happens. That is because the nurseryman uses the plants that have germinated first and breeds from them to obtain more seeds. In fact he is selecting, among other qualities, for regularity in germination; but in nature it is not necessarily advantageous for all the seeds from each harvest to start growing together. It only needs a single disaster, flood or drought or unseasonable frost for the whole generation to be lost and so for wild plants it is exceptional for all the seeds to germinate as soon as conditions become suitable. Some plants, indeed, produce different types of seed. There is a very tiresome weed called fat hen, which produces no less than four different kinds of seed. The largest will germinate almost immediately, the next largest after about six months and the two smallest after longer periods. Indeed one reason for the success of weeds is their ability to remain viable in the soil for apparently unlimited periods. Many country dwellers must have noticed how after ploughing up of old pastures, plants such as poppies, which have not been seen in the district in living memory, suddenly appear in vast quantities in the recently disturbed earth, having lain in the soil for many years until conditions became ripe for germination.

By no means all seeds have a long life. If you find you have some of last year's cabbage and lettuce seeds left over and sow them, you will find that many of the cabbage seeds will germinate, but practically none of the lettuce. Incidentally, the cabbages you get from old seed are not likely to be so good as those raised from fresh seed and it is probably false economy to use this year-old seed, but the point made here is that cabbage seed has a longer life than lettuce seed. It is possible to prolong the life of most seeds by first dehydrating them and then storing them at very low temperatures, but this needs complicated apparatus and is not a practical proposition for the amateur gardener. Generally it is the fresh seed that gives the best results, although there are a few exceptions, most notable for the gardener being the Chinese aster (*Callistephus*) which seems to give better plants that come more rapidly into flower if year-old seed is used.

This may well be the place to describe how a seed is formed. In flowers there is a female element comprising the ovary, in which the ovules are situated and from which an outgrowth known as the *style* protrudes. At the top of the style is the

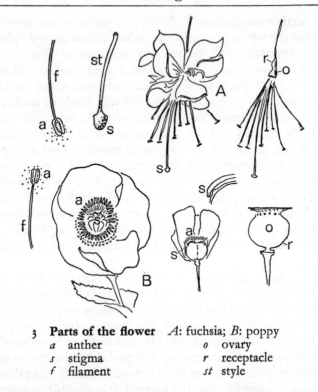

3 Parts of the flower   *A*: fuchsia; *B*: poppy
a	anther	*o*	ovary
s	stigma	*r*	receptacle
f	filament	*st*	style

stigma, which is often covered with a sticky surface, when it is ready to receive the pollen. The male organs are the *stamens*, typically composed of slender filaments at the end of which are sacs, known as the *anthers*, which eventually ripen and open to release the pollen, composed of minute granules, usually, but not invariably, yellow in colour. It is rare for flowers to be fertilized by their own pollen and so usually the anthers and the stigma do not ripen at the same time. One is usually ripe before the other, although which ripens first differs from plant to plant. This ensures that the flowers will be pollinated by pollen from another flower, this is desirable from an evolutionary point of view, but may sometimes be disastrous for the horticulturist if he only has one plant. Numbers of Chinese primulas, often very desirable and ornamental plants, have been temporarily in cultivation but have been lost because it was impossible to get them to produce good seed. In the wild there are plenty of primulas, so that insects can carry the pollen from plant to plant, but if the gardener has only succeeded in raising a single plant he will probably be unable to pollinate the flowers, unless he can find another gardener in the same position. It is the ripening of the stigma that is the important period. It is possible to collect pollen and store it for several months in a dry cool condition (for example by sealing it in an envelope and putting it into the refrigerator), but the stigma only remains receptive for a few days, or in some cases, a few hours. Thus there is a rhododendron known as 'Devaluation' which is a hybrid between R. *arboreum* and R. *auriculatum*. R. *arboreum* flowers in March and R. *auriculatum* in August, so the hybridist has to keep the pollen of R. *arboreum* from March until the R. *auriculatum* comes into flower five months later.

Once the pollen has landed on the receptive stigma it is apparently stimulated by the sugars that the stigma gives off and sends a tube down the inside of the style, which eventually enters the ovule by a small canal known as the *micropyle* and extrudes a nucleus and some protoplasm, which fuses with the nucleus and protoplasm of the ovule. To start with the cells of the pollen grains and those in the ovules contain only half the number of chromosomes that occur in the cells of the parent plants. When the nuclei fuse they bring the two halves together and the fertilized ovule now contains a cell with the full complement of chromosomes. This cell now starts to grow and divide, part forming the plumule and radicle of the future plant, and part forming the food reserve, which can either be part of the cotyledons or remain undifferentiated. As the embryo develops, it becomes much drier. The ovule has as much as 90 per cent of water in it, while the ripe seed has probably less than 10 per cent. At the same time the two coats which surround the ovule harden and often change colour. A well-known example is the pea, where the developing ovule is the vegetable we eat. It is green with a smooth coat, while the

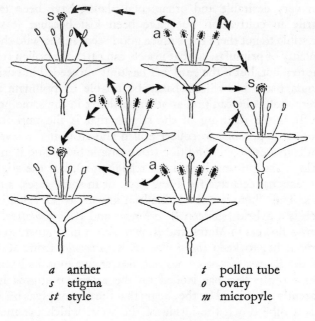

a	anther	*t*	pollen tube
s	stigma	*o*	ovary
st	style	*m*	micropyle

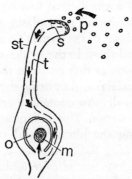

4 Fertilization

In most plants the stigma and stamens ripen at different times so as to ensure cross-pollination and discourage in-breeding. Pollen is not released until the anthers are ripe and pollen will not adhere to the stigma until it is ready.

seed we sow is grey with a wrinkled coat. When the seed is ripe it becomes detached from the walls of the ovary, if it had been attached before. While this has been going on the ovary itself has been changing. First of all it becomes enlarged and its swelling is a sign to the gardener that seeds are being formed. It may also change considerably in appearance in the case of berries, pomes, drupes and other edible fruits. To be accurate, in the case of fruits it is not always the ovary which becomes pulpy, sometimes it is the part surrounding the ovary, known botanically as the *receptacle*. Such is the case with the apple and the strawberry. With stone fruits and berries such as currants it is the ovary itself which becomes pulpy. Other ovaries just enlarge and finally become hard and dry, when they open to release the seeds, sometimes, as we have seen, with considerable violence so as to eject the seeds some distance from the parent.

There are exceptions to practically any statement we care to make about plants and some ovaries never split at all. The hazel nut is a good example. If the nut is not removed from the shell by an animal the shell will eventually rot away, but the plant depends on animals for its distribution. Fruits known as achenes, like those of the strawberry or the buttercup also do not split, but each seed is enclosed in a tight, dry coat, which behaves like an additional seed coat. Moreover, some seeds are still green when they are shed and do their final ripening in the soil. The plant you are most likely to meet doing this is *Anemone blanda*, but this is another tiresome habit of some of the desirable Asiatic primulas, and is yet another reason why they are so hard to bring into cultivation. In the case of the Christmas rose and other hellebores, the seeds ripen in the usual way, but the ovaries remain green, so that it is only too easy to go to collect hellebore seed at the end of May and find that it has already been shed. We shall be looking more closely at seed gathering in Chapter 7, so there is no need to labour the point here.

Normally the seed becomes hard and dry before it is shed from the capsule, but in some cases seed will germinate before it is released naturally, if it is removed when separated, but still green. We have already seen how some Asiatic primulas, *P. sonchifolia* is the best known, disgorge their seeds while they are still green, and it has been found that the seeds of other Asiatic primulas will germinate readily if taken from the capsule while still green. This may well happen with many other seeds and if anyone has time to try sowing immature seeds and noting the results they could make a notable contribution to both horticulture and science. It may well be that seeds that are normally hard to germinate might prove much easier under these circumstances. No doubt most of the experiments would prove failures, but every success would prove an advance in our knowledge.

Once the seed is ripe it will endure many extremes of temperature or climatic conditions. In the 1840s Edward Madden noted seeing plants of *Berberis aristata* at the Dublin Botanic Garden, which had been raised from seeds that he had removed from jam. Probably not all seeds would survive prolonged boiling, but apparently these berberis did. In Alaska seeds of the Arctic lupin (*Lupinus arcticus*) were unearthed from permanently frozen soil and were found to be still viable after what was reckoned to be at least 7,000 years. Nowadays this fact causes less surprise as it has been found that the best way to prolong the life of seeds is to store them in airtight containers at a temperature of −10° C, under which conditions seeds that are naturally short-lived may survive for many years; since the technique is relatively modern we are not sure how long the seeds will remain viable, but a minimum of twenty-five years is aimed at. If the natural moisture content of the seeds is somewhat reduced, the chances of survival seem better. However, there still remain some seeds, most notably nuts such as acorns with a higher than average moisture content, to which this technique is not applicable and the list contains such plants as maples, poplars and willows. It is impossible to remove sufficient water for them to remain viable and if they are frozen without dehydration they are killed by the water freezing. On the other hand suitable seeds of tropical plants, for example many orchids, come to no harm at all if frozen in a dry condition, although the plants would not survive such temperatures for more than an hour or so.

This information, fascinating though it be, is not of much use to the amateur gardener, who will, in any case be sowing his seed in what he hopes will be a reasonably fresh state. It has, however, been found that seed keeps best under cool conditions and so, even if the amateur only needs to keep his seeds for a short time, they will probably survive best if packeted and put into the refrigerator, but not in the freezing compartment. Dry seeds are in a state of suspended animation and the cooling provided by storage in a refrigerator must not be confused with the cooling treatment recommended for some seeds to assist germination. This latter can only take place after the seeds have absorbed water, the first essential preliminary to germination, and it is this aspect to which we had best turn our attention now.

2 Sowing, germination and composts

It is not perhaps too fanciful to think of the seed as the *Sleeping Beauty* and the gardener's task as one of finding the correct Prince Charming to kiss it into life. With most of the seeds that are grown extensively there is no problem. You sow the seeds and, provided conditions are right, up the seedlings come. Other seeds will just lie in the pot or in the open ground and you do not know if they are dead or just sleeping and it is these slower germinating seeds which can cause most problems.

For a seed to germinate it needs water, oxygen and a suitable temperature. This varies from plant to plant. Seeds from the tropics need a high temperature for germination and will not germinate otherwise. When we come to temperate plants we also find that either too high or too low a temperature may prevent germination. In some plants a particular temperature seems to have quite spectacular results, but unfortunately this varies from plant to plant, and for most plants effects are not known, and the variation is not only between genera, but also between species. For example *Gentiana pneumonanthe* responds well to a high daytime temperature. If 25° C is given good germination results with, rather oddly, the best result (81 per cent) being obtained when the night temperature was the same. The willow gentian, *G. asclepiadea*, gave the best germination with a daytime temperature of 25° C, but the night temperature had to drop to 5°. With the conditions that gave the best results for *G. pneumonanthe* only 10 per cent of the willow gentian germinated. Another popular garden gentian, *G. septemfida* showed rather poor germination in all cases, but easily the best was with a day temperature of 20° C and a night one of 10°. Fortunately with most ornamental plants quite a low percentage germination will give one ample plants, so our ignorance of the optimum temperatures for most plants is not so important for the amateur as it would be for the professional nurseryman. What does seem to be borne out by these experiments is that for the majority of plants a difference in temperature between night and day is almost essential. A good average to aim at would seem to be a day temperature of 20° C falling to 10° at night. This is the sort of temperature range which can be expected from an unheated greenhouse in late April and in May. It is not possible for any amateur to maintain the laboratory conditions with which the results I have cited were obtained and it does seem as though even quite trifling variations in temperature can cause the germination percentage to change considerably. A delphinium species was found to germinate best with a day temperature of 15° C and a night one of 5°, but if there was no variation between the night and day temperatures there was no germination at all. Under either greenhouse or outdoor conditions it is very unlikely that the temperature will not fall at night, so this particular hazard may be disregarded for all practical purposes.

With unheated structures it looks as though the best method is to sow the seed in February and just wait patiently until conditions are right for germination. With heated structures one can probably sow a month earlier, while with plants that are being sown outdoors, March is probably quite early enough for sowing. There are some exceptions into which we will go later.

For small quantities of seed there is much to be said for an electric propagator. Basically this is a miniature Wardian case with thermostatically controlled heating cables which maintains an even temperature for the seedlings, while the perspex roof prevents water evaporation. So no watering is necessary between the time when the pots are put in the propagator and the time when they are taken out. There are only two possible snags. Firstly, you have to fill your propagator with seeds that

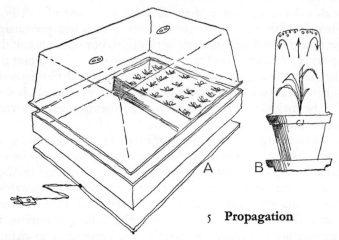

5 **Propagation**

A Propagator case with translucent acrylic cover, receptacle for seed boxes and electrically warmed metal plate below

B A simple plastic cover which can be placed over a flower pot; moisture produced from the surface of the seedling condenses on the cold inner surface and returns to the soil where it is taken in again by the root system, maintaining a humid atmosphere

need approximately the same treatment and that may be expected to have a similar germination time. Secondly, you have to take some additional care when you remove your pots from the propagator. They must be gradually hardened off. It would be fatal to take them straight from the propagator into the open air and they should either be placed in a cool greenhouse or kept on a warm window sill for two or three weeks before they can be exposed to the open air.

Before any germination can start the seed has to imbibe water. With some seeds the outer coat is permeable or soon becomes so in the soil, but others have very hard coats, or are covered with some protective covering like the hawthorn. Here the only direct conduit for water is the tiny pore, the micropyle. In many cases the gardener can overcome these disadvantages. Many growers of sweet peas chip or file away part of the seed coat and the same process must be undertaken in raising camellias from seed. With other seeds, most notably seeds of plants that are designed by nature to pass through the digestive tract of birds or animals, it is necessary to resort to stratification. With large quantities of seeds this entails putting down a layer of damp sand or peat or a mixture of the two, then a layer of seeds, then a further layer of sand, then a further layer of seeds and so on. With small quantities this is rather too elaborate and it will suffice to mix the seeds with the damp sand or peat and put the mixture in a polythene bag.

The stratified seeds must then be exposed to cool conditions. Leaving them out over winter is quite satisfactory, provided you can be sure that mice or other vermin cannot get to the seeds. In nurseries the stratified seeds are often buried in a dry clay bank, but this is by no means always available to the small gardener, although there is nothing to stop him burying the polythene bags. For reasons which are obscure one does not necessarily get the same result if one sows the seeds when ripe in a normal seed compost and leaves the pot out of doors. After the correct stratification period you will get some seeds germinating, but not with the regularity that they usually show after stratification. Many seeds, such as berberis and roses germinate after only six months' stratification and if you have only small quantities, they will pass this period quite happily in the refrigerator, provided they have imbibed water before being exposed to the low temperature. On the other hand seeds of plants such as hawthorns or yews require eighteen months' stratification; that is to say they require two cool periods with a warm period in between. This means that seeds that were ripe, say, in the autumn of 1976, would not germinate until the spring of 1978. Some processes have been suggested to curtail this long pre-germination period, but they are not really practicable for ordinary gardeners like us. Later on we shall be listing plants that require special treatment before sowing, so we need not worry unduly about that at the moment.

The third essential for germination is oxygen, but since this is present in the atmosphere we can take its presence for granted. Given water, oxygen and the correct temperature the seed will germinate and the presence of soil is not needed. But if we wish to grow the seed so that it develops into a plant it is necessary.

A condition essential for a good seed compost is that it should retain moisture adequately, but that any surplus moisture should rapidly drain away. We also require the texture to be such that the young roots can easily penetrate the compost and that this compost will contain sufficient nutrients to maintain the seedling until it is large enough to be transferred to a richer medium. Although there are exceptions, to which we will come later, the best medium has been found to be composed of:

> 2 parts loam
> 1 part peat
> 1 part gritty sand.

The John Innes seed compost adds about 42 g (1½ oz) of superphosphate and about 21 g (¾ oz) ground chalk to every bushel of this mixture. The trouble that the amateur will find is with the first ingredient, the loam. The formula envisages a really fine, slightly acid loam such as might be obtained by stacking turves and leaving them for a year, but such soils are becoming increasingly difficult to find. We may well have to make do with ordinary garden soil, but it is less rich in nutrients and may well have a poor physical structure. This can partly be overcome by adding home-made humus from the compost heap. In order to get the best results the soil should be steam sterilized. This again is usually not possible for the small gardener. Small quantities can be put over a boiling saucepan, but it is probably simpler to put the loam in the oven set at 200° F (about 93° C) and leave it until the centre of the pile has reached this temperature. The loam should be well dried out before being sterilized. The choice between sedge peat and moss peat seems very much a matter of personal likes and dislikes and does not seem to make much difference in the ordinary case. The sand should be coarse and gritty. If silver sand is easily and cheaply available it is certainly the best, but if not a coarse, washed, river sand will do admirably. Sand has no nutrient value whatever and is incorporated solely to make the compost open and rapid draining, so that very fine pit sands are worse than useless as they make the soil liable to become sodden and thoroughly unsatisfactory. If gritty sand cannot be obtained, a very fine gravel, such as that sold for bird fanciers, is preferable to fine sand.

If your loam is slightly alkaline in reaction and you wish to grow lime-hating plants, it is as well to omit the ground chalk and replace it with flowers of sulphur. If the loam is already slightly acid, the small amount of ground chalk does not seem to do much damage, although it is probably safer to omit the chalk.

Sterilizing the soil means that most soil bacteria and fungus spores are killed, so that there is little risk of the seedlings damping off or dying from bacterial diseases in the young stage. Even so it can do no harm to water the soil with a solution of Cheshunt compound directly before sowing. Damping off occurs more frequently if the seeds are sown thickly, so that the fungus can run easily from plant to plant. Sowing the seeds thinly not only prevents the spread of disease, but also ensures more rapid development of the seedlings, so that it is doubly beneficial.

It is also possible to coat the seeds with certain fungicidal powders. These are either blown on the seeds from puffer packs or powder can be put in the seed packet and shaken up with the seeds. However, all your work in sterilizing soil and in applying fungicides can be undone if you do not have clean containers for the soil and seeds, so clean out all pots or other receptacles.

So far we have been speaking of composts with some amount of loam included, but peat-based composts are becoming increasingly popular and have the advantage of being purchased already made up and of being sterile, so that the risk of soil-borne diseases is minimal. There are, however, disadvantages. The formulation is admirable for the early growth of seedlings, but this means that they develop a root system out of proportion to the aerial parts of the young plant, which makes prick-

B

ing the seedlings out difficult to accomplish without damaging their roots thus giving them a check at a time when it is most undesirable. Moreover many of us find that plants that are started in one of these peat-based composts have to be grown later in peat-based composts. This is admirable if you are growing short-lived pot plants, but disadvantageous if you are growing plants that you intend eventually to plant out in the garden. The other disadvantage with these peat-based composts is that they provide an ideal medium on which unwanted mosses and liverworts can grow, which can be fatal in the case of seeds that take a long time to germinate. The whole surface can be covered before the seedlings appear.

If you do sterilize your loam, it is recommended that it be stored from one to three weeks in an airy situation before being used, but many gardeners do not trouble with this, finding that the interval between sowing and germination is usually long enough for the helpful soil microbes to re-establish themselves, which is the object of the three-week resting period. The trouble is that harmful organisms can also reinfect the soil, especially if it is not stored in a clean container. If you do wish to store the sterilized loam, a polythene bag is suitable for small quantities, while a plastic bin will be found adequate for larger amounts. The bin is washed out with disinfectant or household bleach between one batch of loam and the next, or thoroughly washed with plenty of clean water.

So far we have been speaking of raising the seedlings in pots, or pans, or boxes, but a large number of seeds can be raised perfectly well in the open ground. For this you will have to prepare a seed-bed. We have seen that drainage is an important item in the successful raising of seeds, so a well-drained situation is necessary. The soil should be well broken up to a depth of 45 cm (18 in) and if it is too heavy it may well be a good idea to put a layer of broken bricks or some other hard-core at the base of this 45 cm depth. The top 15–20 cm (6–8 in) should be well broken down, the surface texture reduced to a fine breadcrumb-like tilth, and raked smooth and level. Large stones should be removed, but small stones will help to pre-

serve the drainage. It is quite laborious to m
bed, but once it is made it will be good
although you will need to add some balan
other year.

The composts that we have been describing wil.
adequately for the majority of seeds, but there are exceptions.
Rhododendrons and other members of the heather family with
very small seeds do best in pure moss peat, although the following refinement is suggested. At the base of the container put a
layer of lumpy peat; cover this with a 1 cm ($\frac{1}{2}$ in) layer of compost made up of equal parts of loam, moss peat and sharp sand.
Cover this with very finely-sifted moss peat, and water. Then
sow your fine seeds as thinly as possible. They can either be
left on the surface or just mixed with a little more very finely-
sifted peat. Most of the *Ericaceae* require light to germinate, so
the seed should not be thoroughly buried. However, the pot
can now be enveloped in a polythene bag, so that no drying
out can occur, as this can easily kill the tiny seedlings. One
grower raises ericaceous plants very successfully by using
transparent plastic sandwich boxes. Once the seed is sown, the
lid is put on and the seeds and young plants receive practically
no further attention. Being closely fitting there is practically no
evaporation of water, although quite a lot of moisture condenses on the lid. All that has to be done is to lift the container,
tip it slightly, so that this condensation falls back to the soil, and
repeat this operation whenever necessary. It is also necessary to
keep these sandwich boxes out of direct sunlight in the summer,
as otherwise there is a risk of the plants being cooked, but since
rhododendron seedlings must be kept shaded in whatever container they are grown, this makes little difference. The seedlings
are left in these sandwich boxes until they have grown tall
enough to reach the lid, by which time they will be large
enough to prick out, or even to be planted out of doors. This
method works very well for this grower, but my personal experience has been less happy, so it may not be as foolproof as it
sounds. Owing to their minute size it is never particularly easy
to raise plants of the heather family from seed, until they have

made two pairs of leaves. The seed is so dust-like that it is difficult to sow it really thinly. It is best with all seeds to tip a small quantity in the palm of one hand and then pick up a small pinch between the thumb and forefinger of the other hand and release the seeds by moving the tips together.

Both the John Innes and the loamless seed composts are somewhat low in nutrients and the seedlings are only left in them until they are large enough to handle, when they are pricked out in boxes or potted on singly in a potting compost. Moreover, there are some plants that are not moved for at least a year and maybe longer and these must be sown directly into the potting compost. Bulbous subjects are the main exemplar here, as they are particularly resentful of any root disturbance in the early stages and it is easy enough to lose your young bulbs if you try to prick them out during their first season. They are not, however, the only plants that require sowing in a potting compost. At the John Innes Institute, where the formulation of the various composts was worked out, it was found that, cinerarias, cucumbers, tomatoes, and the Christmas cherry all did better when sown direct into potting compost, while, on the other hand, cyclamen did better when they were not only grown but potted on in the seed compost. The John Innes potting compost is made up as follows:

   7 parts (by bulk) sterilized loam
   3 parts peat
   2 parts sharp sand.

To each bushel (a bushel is the equivalent of 8 gallons (36 litres), so 4 two-gallon bucketfuls of soil is a bushel) add 110 g (4 oz) of John Innes Base, which can be purchased already made up and 21 g ($\frac{3}{4}$ oz) of lime or ground chalk or ground limestone. This makes the mixture abbreviated as JIP 1 and is suitable for plants in 7·5 cm (3 in) pots. For plants in pots of 10 and 12·5 cm (4 and 5 in) you double the quantities of chemicals, while for 15 cm (6 in) and larger pots you treble the amounts. These mixtures are abbreviated to JIP 2 and JIP 3. The John Innes base is usually purchased already made up, but if you wish to make it yourself the formula is:

2 parts hoof and horn
2 parts superphosphate
1 part sulphate of potash.

Unlike the soil mixture, the parts here are reckoned by weight. A pound of the mixture would have slightly over 6 oz of hoof and horn and the same weight of superphosphate and a little over 3 oz (75 g) of sulphate of potash. The additional chemicals in JIP 2 and 3 do not necessarily make the plants grow any faster, but they keep the plant going for longer, before any extra feeding is required.

This compost, or its equivalent in loamless formulations, is suitable for the vast majority of plants, but there are a few exceptions. Plants with very fine roots, such as begonias and, once again, many ericaceous plants, require a more open compost and this is obtained, usually, by doubling or trebling the amount of peat. If a supply of leafmould is obtainable, this will do even better than peat, but in the case of lime-haters, such as heathers and azaleas, care must be taken that the leafmould does not come from an alkaline soil. Considerable damage has been observed from the use of mould from beech trees that had been growing on chalk downs.

Cacti and succulents are plants that both require a special compost and that resent root disturbance in their early stages, so that they are sown in the same compost as that in which the mature plants are grown. This usually consists of equal parts (by bulk) of coarse loam, grit and crushed bricks and mortar rubble. This gives a very porous medium. For seed sowing this is topped up with a layer of sharp sand and the seeds are placed on this and watered in. Normally they are not covered, although any rather large seeds should be lightly covered with sand, but, apart from opuntias, most cactus seeds are small. This treatment applies, too, to cactus-like succulents of Africa. Although such plants are inhabitants of deserts, where prolonged drought is frequent, the seeds are programmed not to germinate except when the soil is moist, so that the seed compost should be kept well watered. A temperature of 18–20° C (64–68° F) seems to give the best results for fairly rapid germination and, as with the majority of seeds, spring and early summer is the best time for sowing. Provided that the seeds have not been sown too closely they can stay in the seed pans or boxes for eighteen months, after which they can be potted up separately.

The John Innes Seed Compost, the John Innes Potting Compost and the Cactus Compost are the main bases for seed sowing, with pure peat, or peat and sand, proving most satisfactory for heathers and their allies, but for some subjects some variation is advised by specialist growers. Alpine plants seem to do better with double the quantity of sand in the JIS, especially if they are plants that naturally grow among rocks or in crannies. With these it has also been found advisable to top the surface with a thin layer of coarse grit. The seed is laid on the grit and then watered in with a fine rose, which gets the seed well embedded and it is easy for the little roots to go through the grit into the more nourishing compost. All these variations are worked out by experience and it is not advisable to alter the proportions of loam, peat and sand without some good reason.

Once we have prepared the compost, sown the seed and watered it in, the seed should start to germinate. The first essential is that it should take up water and this normally takes place without any special treatment being necessary. Incidentally, some seeds can take up water even if they are dead, so the fact that a seed has swollen as a result of taking in water is not necessarily an indication that it is viable. If it is alive, once the water has been absorbed the seed, which has been in a state of suspended animation, starts to *come* alive. It starts to take in oxygen, the enzymes in the food reserve are dissolved, so that they can be moved to the embryo plant and then this starts to grow. First the radicle elongates, pierces the seed coat, known as the testa, and penetrates the soil, where it then starts to emit true roots. The purpose of the radicle is not so much to take in nourishment as to anchor the young seedling. Once this has been accomplished the plumule emerges from the soil. The plumule consists of two cotyledons in the case of dicotyledons, a single cotyledon in the case of the mono-cotyledons, and a large number of cotyledons in the case of the gymnosperms, which are mainly conifers. In monocotyledons and gymnosperms the cotyledon is not clearly differentiated from the normal leaf of the plant, but in dicotyledons, the seed leaves are often very different in shape from the mature leaves. Why this should be so is not very clear. It is usually assumed that the seed leaves may have been the shape of the leaves of the original plant before the leaf shape became changed as the result of evolutionary forces. This may well be so and some support for this theory comes from the fact that in the case of plants that are regarded as primitive, as for example, magnolias, there is less differentiation between cotyledons and adult leaves than there is in, for example, a plant like the carrot, where the seed leaves are long and narrow and entire, while the mature leaves are triangular and deeply dissected. Personally, I do not feel that the true explanation for the difference has been found as yet.

Normally the cotyledons emerge from the ground and develop chlorophyll, the substance that makes leaves green, but this is not invariable, as anyone who has grown peas or beans can testify. In these and often with other large seeds, the cotyledons remain underground, still surrounded by the testa and it is the secondary shoot that emerges from the ground and develops leaves and chlorophyll. In the case of dicotyledons, once the cotyledons have emerged they carry between them a bud which, as the plant obtains more nourishment, develops into the main stem of the plantlet and produces the first true leaves, which generally resemble those of the adult plant. There are a few exceptions. Most eucalyptus first produce leaves that are more or less circular and opposite, while later the leaves become sickle-shaped and alternate. Cypresses and some junipers first produce needle-like leaves and later tiny scale-like leaves that are closely set over each other like tiles on a roof and these are called *imbricated*. These are, however, exceptional and generally the first mature leaves differ only in size from any subsequent leaves. As we have seen there is less differentiation in the case of monocotyledons, but sometimes a difference is sufficiently marked. That popular house plant, the Swiss cheese plant (*Monstera*), first produces an entire, more or less heart-shaped leaf. As the plant grows the margin of the leaf becomes more lobed and the lobes are deeper, and after a year or so the characteristic perforations appear. In the same way, if you plant a date stone, the first leaf you will see will be an entire oblong-oval leaf. As the plant grows the later leaves divide into a number of leaflets, but it is quite a few years before you see the characteristic long feathery leaves, divided into many leaflets, of the mature date palm.

Both the radicle and the plumule of the seedling are affected by gravity. The radicle is affected positively, so that it will always grow downwards, the plumule negatively so that it will always grow upwards. This means that it makes no difference to the seed how it falls on to the ground. This is broadly true, but we have seen how erodiums and pelargoniums screw themselves into the soil and it has been found that with flat seeds like cucumbers and marrows it is best for the seeds to be inserted edgeways with the pointed end downwards. Indeed if seeds do have a pointed end and they are large enough to handle individually it is better to see that the pointed end is bottom-most in the soil but this is not really essential. The erodium or the cucumber seed will germinate even if laid flat, but it will expend some unnecessary energy in getting into a suitable position, which means that the plant takes that much longer to develop, which may be a serious matter in the case of the cucumber.

So far we have been assuming that given moisture, oxygen and the correct temperature, the seed will germinate, provided it is viable, but that is not always the case and it is time that we looked at other factors that affect germination.

3 Factors affecting germination

That popular plant for moist situations, *Primula japonica*, has been the subject of many experiments to assess the best way of getting good germination. Various questions required an answer. Should the seeds be sown as soon as they are ripe or should they be dried and kept through the winter and sown in spring? Would the seeds germinate equally well in the light as in the dark? Would some chilling treatment encourage or discourage germination? If it encouraged it, for how long would the seed need to be chilled? With this primula it was found that there was a moderate germination if fresh seed were sown with a daytime temperature of about 20° C and a night-time temperature of only a little less, otherwise germination was bad whether the seed was kept until December or until April. Seeds sown in darkness failed to germinate at all. Up to now the best result had been fresh seed sown at the temperature quoted above which had given a 53 per cent germination. The seeds were now sown in spring and the pot put in an ordinary domestic refrigerator at a temperature of about 2° C. After they were chilled for a fortnight and then put in a temperature of 15° during daylight and 4° at night, a germination rate of 70 per cent was reached and this was slightly improved after four weeks' chilling treatment, while after eight weeks and given a day temperature of 20° and a night one of 15°, 77 per cent germination was obtained. In nature this chilling process is obtained through climatic variations and it is not a bad thing for the seeds to germinate erratically over a long period, some germinating in the autumn from the fresh seed and the rest during the spring, but the gardener would prefer, if possible, to have all his plants germinate together. What seems to happen with many Asiatic primulas (and maybe ones from elsewhere), is that the seed does not necessarily complete its development in the capsule and undergoes what is referred to as after-ripening in the soil. This was particularly marked with another primula, *P. sinopurpurea*, whose seeds germinated very badly if sown when fresh or in December, but gave 84 per cent germination, when sown in April at a temperature nearly constant at 15°. A large number of different primulas were used during these experiments, but very few general rules can be drawn from the results, though generally seed which had been kept for four months germinated better than did seed sown immediately after ripening. A salient example was *P. sikkimensis*, which gave a 29 per cent germination when sown fresh with a day temperature of 15° and a night one of 10°, while seed kept until December and sown in the same temperature gave a 94 per cent rate. It is also fairly clear that light is necessary to give the best germination for primulas. The amount of light required by seeds is not great; development is not inhibited by a light covering of compost, but if light is totally excluded this can certainly affect germination in many cases. On the other hand many seeds germinate better when in darkness and, indeed, this has always been regarded as the general rule. It is the seeds that need light that are exceptional. It is only by experience that one learns to recognize some of these, but it can be regarded as fairly certain that very small seeds will germinate better in light, if only because if sown too deep they would be unable to reach the surface before their food reserves were exhausted. Large seeds probably do better with dark conditions, although the number of seeds that will not germinate in light is probably not very large and is usually confined to desert plants, which have to evolve a number of tricks to survive that plants from more equable regions can dispense with.

It is worth noting that the after-ripening can take place perfectly happily in a seed packet, while the chilling is only effective after the seeds have imbibed water and are in a condition of potential germination. After-ripening is often found in plants from such regions as the Mediterranean or California, where the summers tend to be hot and dry. Seeds from such regions will often not germinate at all at high temperatures and the necessity for after-ripening will carry them through until the autumn, even though the temperature may not be too high during the intervening period and there may be the occasional thunderstorm which could provide the seed with sufficient water.

Even when no after-ripening is known to occur it does seem that with seeds of a normal life span it is best to sow the seed not as soon as it is ripe, but in the following spring. However, this general rule has many exceptions and some seeds, most notably willows, have a very short life and many seeds will die if they are not sown within a week of ripening. Seeds containing a lot of water, such as acorns, hickories and some maples die if they become too desiccated and such seeds are, therefore, unsuitable for storage in a seed bank. Much the same applies to oily seeds such as magnolias and hellebores. These must be sown as soon as ripe, although there is no guarantee that they will germinate particularly quickly. What is certain is that if they are not placed in a moist medium rapidly they will not germinate at all.

In some of the controlled experiments the varying night temperatures seem to make a very significant difference. For example with a day temperature of 25° C (77° F) there was a 42 per cent difference in germination when the night temperature fell to 5° C (41° F) instead of to 15° C (60° F), the lower temperature giving the best result in the case of the willow gentian (*Gentiana asclepiadea*) and this also held good for *G. pneumonanthe* and *G. andrewsii*, although the difference was not so marked (14 per cent and 9 per cent), on the other hand *G. septemfida* did better with the higher night temperature, but it gave the best results when the day temperature did not rise above 20° C (68° F) and fell at night to 10° C (50° F). With such fluctuations unber controlled conditions it is not surprising that gentian seeds are generally regarded as difficult.

Many, such as the favourite *G. acaulis*, never germinate without previous chilling, although this can be effected easily enough, either by sowing outdoors in the autumn and letting the natural low temperatures have their effect, or by sowing the seed and putting the pots into a domestic refrigerator for eight weeks. After this they can be brought into warm conditions and will usually germinate as satisfactorily as gentians ever do. Normally seeds germinate more rapidly in warm conditions, but the temperature can sometimes be too high for some plants of temperate climes. Most delphinium seed does not germinate very well if it exceeds 20° C (68° F), although this would not apply to the Californian or Iranian delphiniums. Quite a few plants, including catalpas and some honeysuckles will not germinate if the temperature rises above 25° C (77° F). Mind you, an occasional rise to this temperature will not inhibit germination, it is only when it is maintained consistently that no germination will take place.

A knowledge of the conditions under which the plant grows in the wild may well be advantageous in giving seeds the best treatment, but it is by no means certain if this is always the case. Let us go back to our willow gentian. The best germination (52 per cent) was obtained with a day temperature of 25° and a night one of 5°, but are such conditions likely to be found by *Gentiana asclepiadea* in the wild? It is a plant of subalpine levels, from 500 to 2000 metres above sea level, although it does not often grow at this highest level. The plant flowers in August and has ripened and shed its seeds by the autumn, so that it must experience chilling conditions during the winter. In the Alps one can well understand that there is a marked fluctuation between day and night temperatures, more marked than in the lowlands, but it must be somewhat rare for a day temperature of 25° C to be maintained consistently. It must be very uncommon for seeds in nature to meet the conditions of a controlled experiment. Probably what happens in the wild is that the seeds germinate rather erratically over a long period and this theory is borne out by the experience of many alpine gardeners who keep their pans of gentian seed for at least three

years, often getting some seedlings every year. From com-
bining our knowledge of conditions in the wild with the
results of the controlled experiment, it looks as though the
best results would be obtained by chilling the seed for eight
weeks and then keeping the seeds by day at a high temperature,
as in a greenhouse, but letting the night temperature be considerably lower, possibly by standing the pots out of doors
overnight.

We have seen that the first prerequisite for germination is for
the seed to absorb water, but some seeds, most notably those
in the pea family, develop very hard coats so that they appear
impermeable to water and there are various contrivances for
overcoming this condition. The simplest method is to file
away a small portion of the seed coat without damaging the
interior; a practice that many sweet-pea growers indulge in.
Actually with annuals of the pea family it is usually not necessary to take any steps, apart from soaking the seeds overnight
in water. This may not work well with longer-lived plants and
an elementary knowledge of botany may prove helpful here.
Plants belonging to the sub-family *Papilionaceae*, the plants
with the typical pea-shaped flower will usually have their coats
sufficiently abraded if they are put in a glass bottle and shaken
vigorously for twenty minutes. On the other hand plants of the
Caesalpinioideae, which includes plants such as cassia with sym-
metrical flowers, as well as the dioecious, petal-less gleditsia and
gymnocladus will take up water perfectly well after being
soaked in absolute ethyl alcohol for seventy-two hours.

We have seen how some seeds must be exposed to a chilling
process before they will germinate and we have emphasized
that the seed must have taken in water before this chilling will
have any effect, but there are a number of seeds, particularly of
the rose family, which require this chilling, but which also have
impermeable coats. These are all seeds that are commonly
distributed by passing through animals and when this takes
place, the coats are sufficiently abraded for the seed to take up
water, but this will not happen with seeds collected from the
trees. There seems only one effective method of making these

coats permeable and this is to give them a prolonged warm treatment in some moist medium. Under laboratory conditions four months at 25° C is sufficient, but in gardening practice the seeds are simply sown and kept either out of doors or in the greenhouse throughout the summer, keeping the medium which they are in moist. Once this hard coat has become pervious, the seed takes in water and then has to undergo the necessary chilling process. What most people do is to gather the seed when ripe and stratify it for eighteen months, which means that seed gathered in the autumn, germinates in the second spring following. It is possible to overcome the impermeability by soaking the seed for seventy-five minutes in concentrated sulphuric acid, but this is so dangerous that it cannot possibly be recommended outside the laboratory. When we come to consider special treatments for seeds we shall be listing the trees and shrubs that require this treatment.

There are some curious seeds which require no chilling to produce roots, but do require chilling to produce aerial parts. These include many viburnums, peonies and some lilies. The seeds are sown in spring in the normal way and, so far as the eye is concerned, nothing happens. However, if you examine the seeds you will probably find that they are making roots. They continue doing this until the autumn and pass through the winter with quite a good root system. After the natural chilling of winter the cotyledons appear in the spring and the plant then continues to grow normally.

Since some lilies produce their seed leaves in the first year, while others wait until the second, this can be rather disconcerting if you do not know what to expect. Although the rule is not foolproof it is a good working assumption that lilies from North America, Europe and the Caucasus are hypogeal, that is to say they only form a bulbil in the first season and do not show leaves until the following year; on the other hand most lilies from Eastern Asia will produce leaves the first year. However, *Lilium auratum* from Japan is one of the two-year lilies. Finally we have some remarkably tiresome seeds which combine almost all the irritating habits of the seeds we have been discussing above. They have what is termed double dormancy. Seeds of this group require sowing in the autumn and given the normal winter chilling; in the spring the seeds start to make roots and a warm period is needed for this operation, a further chilling is then necessary to break the dormancy of the cotyledon, which does not appear until the second spring. It is mainly plants of the lily family that show this characteristic, most notably trilliums, smilacina and, to a lesser degree, plants such as Solomon's seal and lily of the valley. Occasionally these latter produce leaves the first season, giving the impression that writers such as myself do not know what they are writing about. Well, we know all right, but seeds, like most aspects of plant life, are remarkably poor readers and do not always realize what is expected of them. There are other seeds with this double dormancy, but most of them are rare in cultivation. There is an attractive dwarf North American relative of the berberis, known as *Caulophyllum thalictrioides*, which also has this characteristic.

What this means is that seeds of plants with this irritating character must be obtained in the autumn and if you receive them at any other time there is no point in sowing them before the autumn, so they are best stored in cool conditions until this season. Of course this applies also to any seeds that need some chilling before dormancy is overcome. Spring bulbs, such as snowdrops and crocus will only germinate after much of the winter is passed and, as we shall see, the same applies to many alpines.

Apart from taking up much needed room the main objection to seeds that take a long time to germinate is that vermin, either mice or birds, can eat the seeds before they are ready to germinate. That is why we often resort to stratification. With small quantities of seed, which is usually all that the amateur is concerned with, the seed can be mixed with moist sand or peat in a polythene bag, which can be stored after a few days in the domestic refrigerator, without taking up too much room. Equally, the bags can be buried sufficiently deeply to discourage either birds or mice, voles and rats, provided you can remember

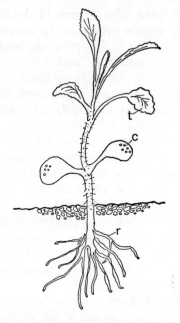

6 **A seedling ready for trans-planting** Note the first true leaves which appear after the dicotyledons
t true leaf
c cotyledon
r roots

where you buried them. Grander gardeners can have a small refrigerator in their potting shed and insert the pots already sown into this refrigerator. In this case it must be remembered that plants that require eighteen months' stratification need to have a warm period between the two cool periods, so the pots must be taken out during the summer and put back in the cool in the autumn. It is shrubs and trees that require this long stratification, so unless you intend to grow hawthorns or snowberries or hollies or yews from seed, you will not have to worry with this.

4 Normal routine

If the last chapter has left you feeling thoroughly discouraged, take fresh heart. The vast majority of seeds will germinate without all this preliminary treatment and in this chapter we will consider the usual way of treating these seeds. February is usually the start of the sowing season, although January has many advantages if you have a heated frame or greenhouse or its equivalent. If you do not have even a warm window sill and intend to grow your seeds outside from the word go, it is probably as well to wait until April before you start. Some vegetables, such as parsnips, are often sown outdoors in February, but with the majority it is best to wait for both the soil and the air to warm up before sowing. If you are sowing indoors you will want to employ some container, either a flower pot or pan or a tray. What you use is chiefly indicated by the amount of seed that you have. With small quantities a pot is probably the best container, but it is possible to have a tray and sow several different varieties therein. With pots an inch of crocks or small stones can be placed at the base of the pot to encourage rapid draining, but with either JIS or a loamless compost the drainage will be quite adequate without this and you will be able in this way to get more compost into the pot, which is advantageous with free-rooting plants. With very small seeds there is probably some advantage in restricting somewhat the amount of compost in the seed container so here the crocks may be employed without fear.

Fill the pots, leaving sufficient space at the top for watering (about 1 cm or $\frac{1}{2}$ in for a 7·5 cm (3 in) pot, twice that for a

49

12·5 cm (5 in) pot and the same for a seed tray), and give the
compost a good soak by immersing the container in water
until the surface is seen to be moist. Ideally you should now
leave it for twenty-four hours, but this is a refinement. Tip the
seeds into the palm of your hand and picking them up in small
amounts with the thumb and forefinger of the other hand, sow
them thinly on the compost. If once you have covered the surface you find you still have seeds left, either return them to the
packet or sow a second container. Do not sow the seeds thickly.
If you have not used sterilized loam or one of the loamless composts, water your JIS with a solution of Cheshunt compound,
made up according to the instructions. If you have minute seeds,
such as begonias or calceolarias, some people recommend mixing them with a pinch of very fine dry sand, so as to obtain a
thinner sowing than could otherwise be obtained. Normally the
seeds are just sown on the surface, but very large seeds can be
pressed into the compost. The normal seeds are then covered
either with a thin layer of compost or with a thin layer of sharp
sand; silver sand is ideal, but expensive. The very tiny seeds are
usually just left on the surface and watered on to the compost
with a very fine rose. The pots or trays are then covered with a
sheet of glass, so as to prevent rapid evaporation if it should
suddenly turn hot. It is possible, also, to envelop the pot in a
transparent or opaque polythene bag, but this must be turned
inside out at regular intervals to remove excess condensation.
At one time people used to save space by cutting discs of
asbestos, so that pots or pans could be piled on top of each
other. This was partly because it was believed that seeds germinated better in the dark, although this is not so widely
believed nowadays. It seems that there are very few seeds that
require complete darkness to germinate and since light is
essential once germination has taken place, it meant that all
these covered pots had to be examined daily and I doubt if
many people use this technique nowadays. Actually, with all
but really minute seeds I doubt if it is necessary to cover the
container at all. Normal seedlings will stand up perfectly
adequately if watered from above with a fine rose, although it

may well be safer from below, once germination is under way. To do this you just hold the pot in a bucket of water so that the level of the water in the bucket is the same as that of the soil in the pot and wait for the water to rise to this level inside the pot—the soil will be seen to be damp. It is not easy to treat seed-trays in this way, so they are best kept for the larger seeds.

If for some reason after watering your young seedlings you find that they have fallen flat, wait for an hour or so and then very gently, with a matchstick or a very small set of tweezers, push the seedlings back into a vertical position. It is usually too strong a stream of water from above that causes the tiny seedlings to fall over. Seedlings left in this condition are almost certain to die, so it is well worth taking the rather fiddly steps necessary to bring the seedlings back to their original position. If you do not have a very fine rose on your watering can, it is probably best to give subsequent waterings from below with any seedlings that show this unsteadiness.

Once the seeds have germinated you want to protect the tender seedlings from direct sunlight, which could possibly burn them. See that on the one hand they do not dry out and, on the other, that the compost is not too wet, and leave them to make their growth until they are large enough to prick out. This is usually when there is one pair of true leaves. This means leaves formed after the initial cotyledons. With the best will in the world it is not easy to avoid damaging the young roots when transplanting seedlings, so with subjects that you intend to grow on in a pot for some time, such as shrubs and trees, it is best to put the young seedlings directly into a small pot. With annuals, biennials and most herbaceous subjects, it is usual to put the seedlings into trays, which can hold up to twenty plants in four rows of five. In any case, with the exception of greenhouse cyclamen, you will be using a potting compost, either JIP 1 (see p. 36) or a loamless potting compost. The young seedlings are usually removed with a thin, slightly trowel-like tool known as a widger, which will lift them out without damaging them. Otherwise they can be loosened with a plant label, and lifted out with finger and thumb, handling

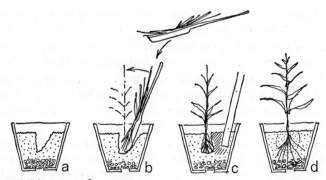

7 **Pricking out:** four stages
  a a hole is formed in the soil
  b the seedling is carried by a widger and carefully raised to the upright position
  c the soil is firmed, using a stick, taking care not to damage the roots
  d soil is reinstated around the stem, and the roots grow out to fill the pot

the leaves only. A hole is then made in the new soil, usually with a blunt stick, which acts as a small dibber, and the seedling is placed therein, taking great care that the seed leaves are only just above the compost surface. The roots must be extended as far as possible. Once the seedling is in position, the stick is inserted close by and pulled towards the seedling, so that the soil is moved firmly around the roots and the young plant is securely anchored. This second hole can be filled loosely with the fingers. If it is possible it is helpful to give the transplanted seedlings slightly warmer conditions for a few days, in order to encourage it to root in the new soil. Once you see the plants growing away again, you can start to give them cooler and more airy conditions and eventually, when there is no risk of frost or of low temperatures, you can harden them off. This entails standing the containers out of doors in a rather shady situation. If you have a frame, this is the best method. The plants are put in the frame, which is at first opened slightly during the daytime; after a week it is opened wider and after a further week the light is removed altogether except during heavy rain or very cold spells. If you have no frame you must just stand the containers out of doors, bringing them under cover if late frosts are expected. I like to let seedlings harden off for three weeks before giving them any further shift. It must be borne in mind that seedlings that have come out of the greenhouse are very tender and succulent and irresistible to slugs, so precautions must be taken against these pests. Sometimes birds can also be a nuisance, so if you can cover the containers with some wire or plastic netting, you will have taken precautions which may be unnecessary, but which are worth taking, as once the birds have pulled the seedlings out, you have little chance of re-establishing them.

Once the seedlings have hardened off and are starting to make fresh growth, they can be moved into the open ground, either into their final situation or lined out in a nursery bed, if it is not convenient to put them in their final positions right away. You do not want to do this if the soil is very cold, or if it is very wet, but usually the beginning of June is a good time for spring-sown seedlings to be put in the open ground. Very small seedlings such as gentians are best kept in their boxes until they are easily visible in the open ground, but growth will be more rapid when they have moved from their containers.

So far we have been talking about spring-sown plants that are started off in warm conditions, but a large number can be sown directly outside. This applies to all hardy annuals and biennials. Most hardy annuals actually make better plants if sown in the autumn; about mid-August in northern Britain and at the start of September in the South, but if that is not convenient they will make perfectly good plants if sown in mid-March or even later. Plants with long tap-roots, such as Shirley and opium poppies transplant very badly and are best sown where they are intended to flower. Although the seeds are minute, they will make larger and more floriferous plants if they are as much as 30 cm (12 in) apart. It is impossible to sow their tiny seeds at the correct distance, so it is a question of thinning out the seedlings as soon as they are large enough. If you have sown in the autumn, this thinning can be left until the following spring. Half-hardy annuals cannot, of course, be sown in this way unless it is proposed to overwinter the seedlings under glass and they are usually left until the spring before being sown. If you have no heating facilities (and the kitchen window sill is quite good enough) you can still get quite adequate plants by sowing outside in late May, after the risk of spring frosts has gone.

Annuals that have been sown out of doors normally need no further treatment apart from seeing that they are kept clear of weeds, but if you have sown the seeds too closely together it is advisable to thin the plants out slightly, as very crowded seedlings can never make good plants. Autumn sown annuals are usually left in the seed bed over winter and put in their flowering positions in early March, although there is no reason why they should not be in their final positions from the time of sowing if that is more convenient. Sweet peas make an exception to this practice in that they are normally sown in pots in October; the pots being overwintered in a frame. Three seeds to a 7·5 cm (3 in) pot is the usual practice; the growing point is nipped out in February and the plants hardened off and put in the soil at the end of March.

Many biennials are sown in the open ground at the beginning of June and this is a particularly good time for plants such as wallflowers, pansies and sweet williams. It is equally good for foxgloves and Canterbury bells, but these have such tiny seeds, that they are usually started in trays, pricked out and eventually planted out. Once the biennials are large enough to handle, they are lifted and planted out, either where they are to flower or in a nursery bed, where they are lined out at distances corresponding to their final dimensions. Thus narrow plants like wallflowers are planted 15 cm (6 in) apart, while plants with spreading leaves or stems, such as Canterbury bells or sweet williams are 22·5 cm (9 in) apart, while some of the giant mulleins (*Verbascum*) may need to be a foot apart. The giant thistle, *Onopordon arabicum*, transplants badly, since it has a long tap-root, so is best sown where you wish it to grow. Fortunately it has quite large seeds, so there is no difficulty about this. Polyanthus, although often treated as biennials, are really herbaceous perennials and so are best treated like other herbaceous perennials and sown in April.

Once your herbaceous plants have been sown, pricked out and hardened off they are ready to go into the open ground. They are still rather small, so it may not be convenient to put them in their final positions, where they could be overshadowed by plants that are adult and well-established, so it is best to line them out in a nursery bed, in the same way that you do the biennials. Lupins have tap-roots that should not be damaged, so it is best to plant the seeds outside in the nursery bed. The seeds are large enough to handle individually, so you can put a seed every 22·5 cm (9 in) apart, putting a few spares in a pot to fill up any gaps. In this case do not wait for the seedlings to make the usual two true leaves, but insert them directly the cotyledons are well expanded. You will find that they have already made quite a long root, which must be put in the soil without being damaged, by making a hole with a dibber and then levering the soil into this hole in the same way as when pricking out. By the autumn or the following spring, whichever is most convenient, these seedlings will have made plants quite large enough to move where you want them to flower. Indeed many will flower in the second summer, although for some you will have to wait one more season. There are one or two subjects which grow very slowly. Peonies, which in any case keep you waiting two years before you see the first leaf, may take anything from four to six years before they flower and they are best kept in the nursery bed for most of this period. The Lenten roses and Christmas roses (*Helleborus* spp.) are also slow-growers, although not so bad as the peonies, and should be about three years in the nursery bed. On the other hand the stinking and Corsican hellebores (*Helleborus foetidus* and *H. corsicus*) may well flower the year after germination, so should be treated like any normal hardy perennial.

At first the treatment is the same for shrubs and trees, but if they are being kept longer than eighteen months before being put in their final positions, they will require yearly moving in the autumn the second year after germination. This will encourage the growth of fibrous roots near the surface and discourage the formation of very deep roots, which would inevitably get damaged if they were allowed to develop, so that the young plants would transplant very badly. This is not necessary with shrubs such as rhododendrons and azaleas, which are naturally shallow rooting and they can be left without disturbance, until they are large enough to be put where they are intended to flower. Many plants of the pea family, most notably brooms, produce a long tap-root and are extremely difficult to move successfully. In fact the seeds are usually sown singly in 7·5 cm (3 in) pots in JIP 1 and, once hardened off, put immediately into their final positions. Fortunately they are rapid growers and a year-old seedling is quite a sizeable plant and may even flower in the second year, although the third year is the more probable.

Apart from bulbs (see Chapter 5) most monocotyledons are treated as other hardy perennials, although they may well have to spend two years in the nursery bed and German irises may require even longer. The main exception are the Californian irises (*II. tenax, douglasii, innominata* and the Californian hybrids). These are all very intolerant of root disturbance when mature, and are put straight into their permanent positions as soon as they are hardened off. The other irises, sibiricas, spurias and germanicas, are treated like hardy perennials. So are hemerocallis and dieramas. Kniphofias, the red hot pokers, make such rapid growth from seed that they can usually go into their final positions in the following spring, but, in general, monocotyledons are slower to mature than dicotyledons, so they tend to spend a longer time in the nursery bed.

Apart from being kept hoed, and watered in dry periods no special attention is required for these young plants. The nursery bed should have been well dug and as much humus incorporated as is obtainable, but otherwise no special feeding is required. Good digging is essential as you want your young plants to make roots freely and they cannot do this if the soil is hard or impacted. Some plants, most notably delphiniums, are excessively attractive to slugs, so it is as well to keep an eye out for these and for other insect pests and take precautions, such as putting down slug pellets and coming out at night with a torch to see the night feeding slugs and caterpillars, and a bucket of salt water, in which they can be killed. Usually plants require little attention once they have got into the open ground, so that you can turn your attention to other matters.

5 Exceptional routines

There are plants in every category from annuals to trees whose seeds need unusual treatments and these will be dealt with individually in the next chapter, but there are also whole categories where the method of raising plants from seed differs to a greater or lesser degree from the basic routine indicated in the last chapter.

ORCHIDS

First among these are orchids, on which I do not propose to say much. The seeds of orchids are dust-like and, unlike most seeds, do not contain a recognizable embryo. In the wild they are entered by the mycelium of a fungus, which supplies nourishment to the mass of cells which form the orchid seed, until it is capable of forming a plantlet and eventually providing its own nourishment. A number of plants, especially in the heather family, depend on their roots associating with fungi for much of their nourishment, but at least the seeds can germinate on their own. This is only possible with orchids if elaborate apparatus is brought into play and raising orchids from seeds is a very specialized business, in which the seeds are raised in flasks of agar and supplied with a special nutrient solution. This all has to take place under sterile conditions and a commercial establishment raising orchids looks more like a laboratory than a nursery and requires apparatus and techniques that the normal amateur cannot hope to obtain. It is by no means certain that these techniques, which satisfy most tropical orchids, would be found to work as well with orchids from temperate climes, which tend to be terrestrial, while most tropical orchids are epiphytic. Still growers did manage to raise orchids from seeds before these elaborate techniques were devised and they did this by putting the seeds around the base of a growing orchid of the same species, or at least the same genus. Since the growing plant would already contain the essential fungus, this would also be present in the potting soil and seedlings were quite often obtained in this way. Unfortunately, some of the tuberous orchids of temperate regions spend quite a time underground forming their first tuber before any leaves are produced. It has been claimed that the burnt orchid (*Orchis ustulata*) grows for fourteen years before it produces its first leaves, although one would like to see this experiment repeated, as it sounds an impossibly long time. In some gardens the soil is naturally rich with *Rhizoctonia*, the fungi necessary for temperate orchids, and self-sown orchid seedlings may appear quite frequently. It will be appreciated that this is quite fortuitous and there is, as yet, no reliable way of raising temperate terrestrial orchids from seed, although a lot of valuable work is being done on the matter and it may soon be as easy to raise temperate as it is to raise tropical orchids. It is essential from the conservation point of view that this be done, as some natural stocks, especially of the hardy cypripediums (slipper orchids), are being dangerously depleted. Still, as I have said, raising orchids from seed is not possible for the normal amateur and need not detain us longer.

As we saw in the last chapter the normal routine is to germinate the seedlings in a seed compost and transfer the seedlings to a potting compost as soon as they are large enough to handle, but there are at least two categories of plants that fiercely resent any disturbance to their roots in the young stages and if this takes place they are liable to die. These are succulent desert plants and many bulbous subjects and both these therefore are treated quite differently.

CACTI

We have already mentioned the compost that is used for raising cacti from seed: equal parts of loam, and crushed brick, to which lime, best in the form of old mortar rubble, is added and some growers also like to add charcoal. This is topped with a layer of silver sand or some other sharp sand and the seeds scattered thereon and watered in. Provided the seeds are sown sufficiently thinly, the plants can be left *in situ* until they are sufficiently large to be potted individually in small pots, usually a matter of two years. If they are too crowded it is possible to lift and replant but in this event they should all be replanted in a larger container, so that there are sufficient roots to prevent the plants being too wet and rotting. It is necessary to keep the plants growing all through the summer, so the compost must be kept moist, but if it becomes over-wet the young plants will suffer. With the coming of autumn, provided the plants have made sufficient growth, they can be kept much drier and during winter only enough water is given to prevent the young plants from shrivelling. The compost is suitable for desert cacti and the succulents from the deserts of South Africa, but the so-called leaf cacti (*Epiphyllum*, *Schlumbergera* and their allies) re-quire rather more loam in the compost, and twice as much would probably not be excessive. They also benefit from the addition of some leafmould, as in nature they are either epi-phytes or woodland plants.

Cactus seeds seem to germinate at almost any time, provided a temperature of 18–20° C (66–70° F) is given, but the most successful results are obtained from seeds that germinate in the spring, as they have the whole of the summer to make some growth and so will be better equipped to face the winter. Un-fortunately, some seeds take rather a long time to germinate and where this is known, there is much to be said for sowing the seed somewhat earlier than April. Opuntias are particularly bad in this respect. The seeds of most succulents are pro-grammed to germinate as soon as they find themselves in the presence of moisture, so that one would expect germination to be fairly prompt in most cases. However, the seeds are also programmed not to germinate all at once, in case the tem-porary wet period is followed by a prolonged drought, which would be fatal to the young seedlings. As a result germination tends to continue over quite a long period and, although most seeds may be expected to germinate fairly soon after sowing, others may mark time so that you will get some more seedlings after a few months and maybe others will wait a year. This is irritating for commercial growers, but probably will not worry the amateur unduly, provided he gets sufficient plants to fill his needs.

An alternative seed compost for cacti is made up of
  2 parts sterilized loam
  1 part sedge peat
  1 part gritty sand
  1 part crushed brick.
If crushed brick is not obtainable, it can be replaced by crushed clinker (not fine powdery ash which would impede drainage), but this must be weathered for six months before it can be used safely. It might well prove toxic if fresh ashes or clinker were used. When the plants are large enough to be potted up separately another suitable compost is made up of equal parts of sterilized loam (which can be replaced by ordinary garden soil, as cacti do not require a rich medium), sedge peat and gritty sand. Some people recommend potting on South African succulents in a rather richer mixture made up of
  3 parts sterilized loam
  2 parts sedge peat
  3 parts gritty sand
  ½ part brick or ash dust.
All these mixtures are improved by the addition of two tablespoonfuls of carbonate of lime (chalk) to every two-gallon (10-litre) bucketful of the compost (or alternatively a teaspoonful to every 15 cm (6 in) potful).

As with most greenhouse plants the water should be at the same temperature as that of the atmosphere in the greenhouse and with cacti and succulents it is best to water from below, by dipping the box or pot in which the seedlings are to about half its depth. If the seeds have been sown so thickly that the young plantlets touch each other, they will have to be pricked out at a suitable distance into another box, but it is far preferable to leave them without disturbance until large enough and with a sufficient root system to go into a 5 cm (2 in) pot and to be potted on when they become larger.

BULBOUS PLANTS

Bulbous plants are another category resenting root disturbance in youth, and since they all have fairly sizeable seeds, they are reasonably easy to deal with. As they are going to remain in their containers for at least a year and in many cases for two or three years they are sown in a potting compost; JIP 1 or JIP 2 or a loamless potting compost all appear equally satisfactory. Since a depth of soil is necessary, the seeds are put in pots and provided there are sufficient seeds a 12·5 cm (5 in) or 15 cm (6 in) pot is the most satisfactory. The seeds of spring-flowering bulbs, crocus, snowdrops, tulips, scillas, and so on, are sown in the autumn and either left out of doors or given the cool treatment in a refrigerator. They germinate at much the same time as their parents are producing their leaves. Thus crocus will probably germinate in February, while tulips will not appear until later. Incidentally, although drainage crocks are not normally necessary with well-made composts, it has been found that they are advantageous when growing bulbous plants, as they discourage the production of long contractile roots, which are mainly designed to pull the bulb down in the soil to a suitable depth, and encourage the growth of fibrous roots, which are the ones that gather nourishment.

Summer flowering bulbs, which originate mainly in South Africa or in Mexico might even be damaged by frost treatment and are sown in spring in the normal way. This, indeed, applies to all South African bulbs, even if they are spring-flowering.

Bulbous seeds usually germinate well (although not necessarily very rapidly), so that the number of seeds you put in a pot will depend on the eventual size of the bulb. For example, you can satisfactorily grow a dozen freesias in a 15 cm (6 in) pot. In this case fill your pot with your compost, firm down, sow twelve seeds, evenly spaced out, about 1·5 cm ($\frac{1}{2}$ in) deep, in April. Cover and water well in. With a temperature around 18° C (65° F) the seeds will germinate in about three weeks. Once they have germinated you can make a second sowing to get a succession of flowers, as the freesias will flower, if you are lucky, from the following October. The seedlings are kept under cover until there is no risk of frost and then, in June, they are brought outside and put in a position that is well-lit, but not exposed to too much direct sunlight until the autumn, when they are brought under cover again. At this stage they need as much light as can be obtained, but must not be too warm; a temperature of 10° C (50° F) is quite warm enough and lower temperatures, provided they are above freezing point, will do no harm. Flowers may well be produced in October if the seeds are sown early enough, but from November to February is the period when flowers may usually be expected.

Although very few bulbs will flower the same year as they are sown, like freesias, the routine is much the same for most bulbous seeds, although for the moment we will disregard lilies, as they need rather special treatment and we will come to them later. With most bulbs, space the seeds well out in the pot and only put enough seeds in each pot to end up with a balanced potful. Thus with snowdrops, six seeds in a 7·5 cm (3 in) pot or a dozen in a 12·5 or 15 cm (5 or 6 in) pot will be found satisfactory and this applies to any small bulbs, such as scillas, crocus, chionodoxas, etc. You may well be asking, since the seeds are kept out of doors in the winter, why they should not be sown in open beds. This is purely a matter of convenience. The first seed leaves are remarkably like grass in appearance and could easily be mistaken for weeds and destroyed, while after the first year the tiny bulbs that have formed are wildly attractive to mice and are easily lost. Even so many gardeners have found that some bulbs manage to sow themselves around without excessive damage. Anyone who grows *Crocus tommasinianus* may well find self-sown seedlings coming up all over the place, so there is evidently no real objection to sowing the seeds out of doors, provided you have such a large number that you can contemplate some losses without regret.

Generally the seedling bulbs behave like their grown-up parents and die down at a suitable period, after which they must be kept dry until the season comes round to start them into growth again. During this resting period it is possible to repot the tiny bulbs, if you consider they have been too crowded, but there are exceptions. Narcissus and lilies scarcely ever rest; the leaves may have died down but the roots are still active and since disturbance is often fatal for young bulbs, it is best to leave these untouched for at least two years and three is even better. Here again lilies provide some exceptions. It is quite possible for *Lilium regale* to flower in the second season from germination, while there are forms of the rather tender *L. formosanum* and *L. philippinense* which may flower after eighteen months. Quite different are some South American irids, such as *Tigridia*, *Cypella*, *Herbertia* and *Rigidella*. These quickly make very large bulbs and usually do require repotting in the second spring, after which a good many will flower. Fritillaries, apart from those with very large bulbs such as *Fritillaria imperialis, pallida, persica* and *raddeana* are usually left in their pots until they flower, even though this may take as long as five years. Since the soil tends to become somewhat exhausted during this period, about a third is removed when the bulbs are dormant and fresh compost given. This operation is usually done in the early autumn and takes place yearly after the first two years.

Plants with quite sizeable bulbs, such as daffodils and tulips, usually take five years or more to reach flowering size, but are best planted out after their third year in the pot. By this time the bulbs are sufficiently large to be unpalatable to mice, while the foliage is distinct enough not to be mistaken for weeds. Indeed it may be possible to do this after the second year and this applies to any other hardy bulbs. Once they are large enough and the foliage is sufficiently differentiated they will probably do better in the open ground. As we know to our cost, many small bulbs will fall prey to mice and squirrels even when of flowering size, so when putting out your baby ones it is best to toss them up in red lead or sprinkle them with paraffin, which will at least discourage the mice in their first season. It seems odd, but it is always the newly planted bulbs that the vermin go for. After a season in the garden they seem to absorb something from the soil that makes them less attractive. There seems no logical reason for this, but I think many gardeners will agree with this observation.

Lilies always seem to provide exceptions to any tentative rules we may make about bulbs and this applies too when growing them from seed. As we have seen, most European and American lilies only make roots in the first season after sowing in the autumn and do not produce any leaves until the second year. Among these is the Turk's cap lily, *Lilium martagon*, but this is sometimes extremely slow to germinate at all and may be in the pot for three years before the first leaves appear. This is not necessarily the case, but it is as well to be prepared for this to happen. The pots can spend all their time out of doors,

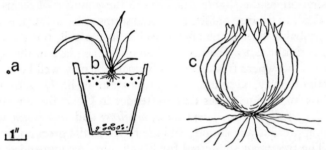

8 **Lilies can be grown from seed:** the bulb will grow to full size after two or three years
a a seed; *b* a seedling about two months old; *c* a fully grown bulb

so the space they take up is not necessarily a problem, but the soil does require to be kept moist in the summer, in case there are invisible but active roots about. The giant lily (*Cardiocrinum giganteum*) is another lily which may take several years to germinate and since it may then take a further seven years to reach flowering size it is not a favourite subject with impatient gardeners.

C

When the two-year lilies are making their roots in the first year they are also making a small bulb and by the end of the next year there is little apparent difference between those lilies which produced leaves in their first season and those which waited until the second spring. At this stage some lilies, notably *Lilium regale* and *L. pumilum* are ready to go into their permanent positions. They should be planted out as soon as the foliage has died down, although great care must be taken to keep the roots without damage and, provided the plants are not too crowded, it is probably best to put the soil ball in the open ground without disturbing the small bulbs at all. This is also the procedure recommended for other lilies, except that they are usually kept a further year in their pots, before being transferred to the open ground. There are some people who sow quite thickly and lift each seedling the moment it germinates and either insert it singly in a small pot or put a few well spaced out in a larger container. This is a rather delicate operation, as the slightest damage to the young root seems to be fatal. In the case of lilies fresh seed seems to be advantageous. It probably does some after-ripening in the soil, but there is some doubt as to whether this can also take place in the seed packet, so where fresh seed is obtainable it may well be sown straight away, although no germination is likely until the following spring. Lilies that are tender in Great Britain, such as *LL. philippinense, formosanum, nepalense* and *sulphureum* will not appreciate any chilling and are raised in the greenhouse.

The treatment suggested for lilies is also recommended for their near allies, notholirion, nomocharis and the larger fritillaries. Notholirions are best treated as cool greenhouse subjects, although they seem to do best if planted out in a greenhouse border and might do equally well in a cold frame. They survive outdoors, but rarely flower. The lovely nomocharis seem to do well in districts with ample rain during the summer and are apt to be unsatisfactory in eastern and southern England.

Alstromerias come very readily from seed, but they have very long roots and are best sown in quite sizeable pots, in which only two or three plants are allowed to survive. Here again if you lift seedlings immediately they have germinated they can usually be transplanted without loss. They need some heat to germinate and are not sown until the spring when they may take anything from three weeks to two months to germinate. If the seedlings are being transplanted they are best put singly into a 7·5 cm (3 in) pot and, once this is full of roots, potted straight on into a 15 cm (6 in) pot, in which each can be left to flower. The hardy species can be planted out either in the autumn or, probably better, in the following spring. Many of the new species introduced from the Beckett, Cheese and Watson expedition to the Chilean Andes, seem to have practically no resting period and are usually producing their new growths in the autumn, so it would seem that a cold greenhouse or cold frame is the best place in which to grow them. They must get some frost in the Andes, so high temperatures are not necessary. Just how hardy they will prove outdoors in our curious climate must await the result of experiments. It is interesting that these plants from the southern hemisphere have no trouble in adapting to the reversal of the seasons if raised from seed, while plants brought back from beyond the Equator tend to follow the rhythm they are used to, which makes spring start in October, and they are extremely difficult to acclimatize to the reversed seasons. This is one reason why plants from the southern hemisphere do best in the northern hemisphere when they can be raised from seed. Once the new seasonal rhythm has been established, seeds or cuttings from these acclimatized plants will continue to follow this rhythm. It is only the original introduction which is most easily effected by growing from seed. Unfortunately, this is not always straightforward, especially with plants not previously known in cultivation. In the Andes there are many species of violets, which make a neat little rosette of leaves and from which the violet flowers emerge in a neat little circle. They are extremely attractive alpine plants. The latest Andean expedition brought back ample seed, of which quite a large percentage germinated, yet, so far as I know, no one has managed to bring a plant to a flowering stage. It is almost always plants from the mountains that seem to present these difficulties and, so far, there seem to have been no problems with bulbous subjects.

It is generally assumed that a very long wait is necessary between the sowing of seed and the appearance of the first flower of a bulb, but this is not necessarily true and in Chapter 9 I shall be listing a number of bulbous plants that will come into flower as soon as many herbaceous plants and, since we usually need more bulbs to make a show than we do herbaceous plants, it is well worth the trouble to raise these from seed. As a general rule it may be assumed that the larger the bulb, the longer it takes the plant to attain flowering and it is true that subjects such as daffodils and other narcissus, tulips and hyacinths may take anything from five years (usually about seven years) before they flower from seed. In any case most of these plants are best known as hybrids and cultivars and would not come true from seed anyway, so your choice is limited to the wild species. Of course if you are sufficiently ambitious you can always make your own crosses, as described in Chapter 8, but there is no point in sowing the seeds of garden narcissus or tulips in the hopes of getting more of the same kind. In this case you have to start by purchasing bulbs, which you can then increase by the offsets which are produced. Daffodils and narcissi can usually be left for a few years before the clumps are lifted and divided, but tulips are best lifted yearly, as soon as the leaves begin to yellow, and hung up in a dry airy place and, once the foliage has dried up altogether, the bulbs can be stored in a warm, dry place, until they are replanted in November. The offshoots are rather small and, if space allows, are best planted in rows in a nursery bed for their first season and then the larger bulbs will probably flower in the next season. We are, however, straying from the subject of seeds.

AQUATICS

Aquatic plants are very rarely raised from seed. This is indeed necessary with new hybrid water-lilies but practically none of these seem to have been raised since the start of the century. Otherwise it is so easy to propagate most aquatics vegetatively that seed is rarely resorted to. If, however, you wish to attempt this rather difficult feat there are certain points to be borne in mind. Generally speaking the seeds should be kept in water before being sown. This should not be necessary for plants that stick to the shallows, such as the flowering rush, *Butomus umbellatus*, and it is certainly unnecessary for waterside irises, such as the handsome *I. laevigata*, whose seeds can be stored in the ordinary way. It is a moot point whether you sow the seeds in a standard seed compost or standard potting compost, but what you most certainly need is a waterproof container in which to stand your pots. With true aquatics, such as water-lilies, water hawthorn or water violet (*Nymphaea*, *Aponogeton* and *Hottonia*) the container should be filled with water until there is 5 cm (2 in) water above the tops of the pots. The temperature of the water should not fall below 15° C (60° F) and may, with advantage, be slightly higher. With the water-side plants it seems to help if the soil is in a state of constant moisture and they can be placed in the container with the water level just below the soil surface in the pots. As soon as they are large enough to handle, the seedlings are potted up separately in very small pots and progressively potted on, while the level of water above the plants is gradually increased until the plants are large enough to be put in your pond.

Water-lily seeds are rarely set and when they are they only float for twenty-four hours, after which they sink and are lost, so keen observation is necessary. Most of the hybrids are sterile and those that have set seed have shown no variation in the first generation. It may well be that the second generation might prove more interesting, but no one seems to have tried and since there is usually a wait of some five years between sowing the seed and seeing the first flower one can see why. It could, however, be interesting, and perhaps profitable, for an amateur to try growing on second generation water-lilies, but to do this he would require plenty of water in his garden.

6 Special treatments

So far we have been acting on the assumption that sowing seeds in spring in warmth will induce fairly rapid germination, although it is realized that in some cases this may be spasmodic and take place over a long period. This is a fairly safe generalization from which to work, but there are exceptions. For example, if you save your own seed or obtain some from a neighbour's garden, should you keep it until the spring or should you sow it at once? We have seen how some seeds require a period of low temperatures before they will germinate, so it is clear that these at least should not be sown in the spring, but in the autumn. A number of plants that require this chilling treatment are known, but is there any way of determining whether it is necessary or not if no information is available? Well, quite a lot can be inferred if you know the conditions under which the plant grows in the wild. It is a fairly safe assumption that plants from high up in the mountains or from regions where severe winters are generally experienced will appreciate winter chilling. There appear to be some exceptions. No increase in germination was noted when chilling was applied to the seeds of that lovely pink azalea with the terrifying name of *Rhododendron schlippenbachii*, although it is native to Korea, with its very bitter winters, and the same applied to *Arenaria groenlandica*, although one would have assumed that any plant from Greenland would want considerable chilling. Mind you, chilling did no harm to the seeds, but they appeared to germinate just as well without it. Still it is a safe rule that in case of doubt sow seeds in autumn when the wild plants come from districts where prolonged winter cold is to be expected. On the other hand in districts such as California, the Mediterranean or South Africa, prolonged frost is rare and chilling the seeds might well be ineffective, or even dangerous, unless the plants are found high up in the mountains. For example, *Anemone blanda* is common in Greece, but always at a considerable height, where the ground is frozen and snow-covered in the winter, so that the seed will appreciate winter chilling, although if one was only given Greece as its native land, one might assume it to be a Mediterranean plant. Similarly, many lewisias come from California, but again they are montane plants and chilling certainly helps the germination of *Lewisia rediviva*, although it does not seem to have much effect with other species. Sometimes there appears no rhyme or reason for the effectiveness of cold treatment. There are two perennial flaxes, which are found in near-Mediterranean conditions, often growing together. The seeds of the blue *Linum narbonense* germinate perfectly well if sown in spring, while those of the pinkish *L. viscosum* require winter chilling before they will germinate well, although even then they germinate very slowly.

Although a working principle can be given as to whether seeds require a cold treatment or not, it seems quite impossible to decide whether it is best to sow fresh seeds at once or keep them until the following spring. Fresh seeds of *Primula japonica* germinate fairly well, but with the seeds of *P. sinopurpurea* the results are very disappointing, while if you keep your seeds until April you will get good germination of *P. sinopurpurea*, but poor germination of *P. japonica*. If, however, you keep your *P. japonica* seeds and sow in early spring and leave for four weeks in the refrigerator, you will again get good germination. Seeds are, of course, sown freshly in nature, but there may be physical reasons why they should not germinate at once. In the Mediterranean, for example, the soil is liable to be so dry when the seeds are shed that no germination is possible until the autumn rains come, even though the seeds may have been shed in May or June. If we sow seeds of Mediterranean plants when they ripen and keep the compost moist we are giving the seeds conditions quite different from those they have in the wild. It seems rather sad that one should have to have a knowledge of geography and climatology in order to germinate the so-called difficult seeds and fortunately in many cases one can learn from other people's experience, provided you know where to find it. Usually with fresh seed one has a good supply, so, in case of doubt you can sow half as soon as it is ripe and keep the other half until the spring. It may well be that the results you get are of great interest, so it is well worth your while to make notes of the amount of germination you get on each occasion (this need not be an actual count, but simply whether the germination was good, moderate or bad), and also of the time that elapsed between sowing and the first cotyledons appearing. It is amazing how little we know of the conditions necessary for good germination of an enormous number of plants.

Yet another aspect which requires consideration is the necessity for light or darkness to bring germination about. It is probably a good working rule that small seeds should be either sown on the surface or very lightly covered. Even with a light covering enough illumination gets through to the seeds to trigger germination, if light is what they need. On the other hand most large seeds seem to do better if planted more deeply. The old gardener's rule that a seed should be buried at a depth three times its diameter was arrived at through observation. Even so there do seem to be exceptions. Apparently both *Nigella sativa* and *Phacelia tanacetifolia*, although their seeds are not particularly large, will only germinate in darkness and there are, as we have said, some desert plants, such as the colocynth, which require to be buried deeply before they will germinate, but the majority of small seeds either need light or are indifferent to it. Very large seeds such as acorns or hazel nuts certainly do better when buried quite deeply and the same applies to broad and scarlet runner beans

We have seen how, in the wild, it is not necessarily advantageous for all seeds to germinate together, even though conditions may appear ideal, and seeds of wild plants that are not in general cultivation will often behave in the same way. So, provided that there is enough room, there is much to be said for keeping your seed pans for at least two years, if you are dealing with seeds whose behaviour is not known. Some plants are known to take a long time to germinate; *Saxifraga aizoon* for example. Usually it will be found that such seeds of temperate plants require a period of chilling before they will germinate, but even after this they may still germinate slowly, and chilling is not always a necessity for slow germinating seeds. *Senecio greyi* does not require any chilling, indeed it should probably be guarded from excessive cold, but the seeds are still very slow to germinate. Although it is helpful to know the wild conditions under which the plant grows, it is not always a reliable guide. The Iceland poppy (*Papaver nudicaule*), for example, requires no chilling and actually germinates best if given some artificial heat, which is not the behaviour one would expect from an Arctic plant. *Silene acaulis* and *S. alpestris* are frequently found growing together, yet chilling is essential for *S. acaulis* and unnecessary for *S. alpestris*.

Various industrious people have assembled facts to suggest the best methods to get the best germination of a number of varieties and the rest of this chapter will be devoted to listing these special treatments. There are, however, still a very large number about which we know singularly little and more information is urgently required.

Annuals and biennials

One would not normally expect much trouble with the seeds of either annuals or biennials, although they may well produce seeds of varying kinds to give a staggered germination. The seeds of the most popular annuals have been selected so long for rapid and regular germination that very few require special treatments. Among the few are beetroots. These germinate better if the seeds are soaked in water for twenty-four hours before sowing. The surroundings of the seed coats contain

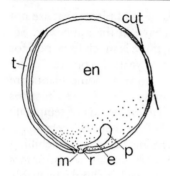

9 **Seed chipping:** the outer skin or testa of this sweet pea is filed or cut to allow moisture to enter the inside of the seed, hastening germination. Care must be taken not to cut through the embryo, which will produce the cotyledon when development begins

e	embryo	*p*	plumule
r	radicle	*m*	micropyle
t	testa	*en*	endosperm

chemicals which inhibit germination, but these are water soluble, so that a good soak will remove most of this inhibitor and the seeds will germinate more rapidly and better. Parsley, although easy enough to grow, will only germinate if the temperature is 15° C (60° F) or higher, so it is no use sowing parsley in cold weather. Among the ornamentals some growers chip the seeds of their sweet peas before sowing and the same is sometimes done for the morning glories (*Ipomoea rubro-caerulea* and *I. purpurea*). With fresh seed this is usually unnecessary, but it may well be advisable with old seed. Incidentally the main trouble with *I. rubro-caerulea* is not so much the germination as providing an equable temperature once germination has taken place. If the day temperature falls much below 20° C (68° F) and if the night temperature fluctuates too much, the young plants are liable to become chlorotic, and produce unhealthy looking, cream-coloured leaves instead of nice green ones. Higher temperatures will usually bring the plant back to a healthy condition, but it will never make as good a plant as one that has been growing steadily throughout its life.

One unexpected phenomenon that has been noted by many growers is that antirrhinum seedlings thrive much better in composts where the loam has not been sterilized. It may well be that the sterilized soil is too rich in nitrates for the young seedlings, which seem to outgrow their strength. So with antirrhinums it is best to use unsterilized loam if you are using the JIS mix and to water the seeds well in with Cheshunt compound or some other suitable fungicide. I have not heard of any trouble with the loamless seed composts.

Herbaceous plants

This is the area in which we have least knowledge and there are some subjects, such as dicentra and corydalis, which prove remarkably recalcitrant. It has been suggested for corydalis, that it behaves like some of the rhizomatous anemones. With these the embryo does not develop until after the seed has been shed, so, presumably a fairly long warm period is necessary for this. This has to be followed by a cool period and the seeds should then germinate in the spring. This warm period needs to take place with the seeds in the soil, so it is evidently best to secure these seeds as soon as they are ripe, although no plants can be expected until the following spring. The same rule will also apply to helleborus seeds which should be sown as soon as gathered, although this does not necessarily mean that plants will be produced very quickly. Germination is usually fairly rapid with the paniculate species *H. foetidus* and *H. corsicus*, but with other species little can be expected until the following spring. This is at least an improvement on peonies, which also seem to do best if fresh seed is used. These are best sown in the autumn to have a preliminary chilling, but, as we have already seen, the seeds only produce roots in their first season and it is only after the second chilling, that the first leaves are seen. Since you then have to wait another five years before you see the first flowers, it will be appreciated that raising peonies from seed is not for the impatient, and it may also explain why the plants are so expensive. Other subjects which need sowing as soon as the seeds are ripe are codonopsis and pulsatilla. I am not sure how essential this is for codonopsis, as I have quite often had satisfactory germination of some species from seed that was not sown when fresh, but purchased from seed merchants in the spring. On the other hand I have always failed with *C. vinciflora*, so probably fresh seed is the best for that. At Bressingham Gardens they find that plants with hard, shiny seeds, such as aquilegia, dictamnus, ranunculus, thalictrum, trollius, tiarella and saxifraga all do best if sown outside in autumn and given the frosty conditions of winter outside. They find that it is necessary to protect the seeds and the seedlings from birds, so it is as well to be warned by their experience. I have not found that this chilling is necessary for all aquilegias, although one would expect it to be necessary for the mountain species. Yet in notes on the germination of alpines provided by Dr. John Good and other members of the Alpine Garden Society, to which we shall come in more detail in the next section, no cooling was found to be necessary in any of the eighteen species for which records existed. On the other hand fresh seed was found to be decidedly better in several instances, while many species germinated better if given gentle heat in the spring.

It had certainly never occurred to me that aquilegia seeds were hard to germinate. I have always sown out of doors in April and always seem to have got a fairly satisfactory germination, so they cannot normally be regarded as difficult seeds.

On the other hand both dictamnus and trollius are usually beasts to germinate and ranunculus may prove tricky and in these cases the winter freezing is almost certainly beneficial.

Member of the pea family are notorious for having very hard seed coats. The everlasting pea, *Lathyrus latifolius*, produces two kinds of seed; those with soft coats germinate fairly rapidly, while those with hard coats can lie in the soil for a considerable time without any sign of life, although they will eventually germinate, long after one has given up all hope. Many growers file away at these hard seed coats, but I have found that most will germinate after being soaked for twenty-four hours in warm water. Some people pour boiling water on to the dry seeds and leave it to cool, while others put water at around 38° C (100° F) into a thermos flask and leave the seeds in that. The trouble with filing or chipping the seeds is that it is so easy to damage the interior, but if this is performed with sufficient care it is usually satisfactory. The object is to ensure that the seeds absorb water, which the hard, impermeable coat tends to prevent. In the soil this hard coat breaks down very slowly. We have already seen how some people recommend shaking the seeds in a glass bottle for twenty minutes, which seems to be effective, but which is extremely tiring. You have no idea how long twenty minutes can seem, while you are shaking a glass bottle vigorously.

Almost certainly there must be other herbaceous plants that need some special treatment, but either the information is not available or I have failed to detect it.

Alpines

On the other hand, thanks to the work of Dr. John Good and members of the Alpine Garden Society, there is a lot of very valuable information on the germination of alpines from seed, which can be found in Vol. 43, pp. 249 ff. of the *A.G.S. Bulletin*. Here we have information as to whether germination is usually good, moderate, or poor as to whether the germination time is less than a month, from one to three months or longer than three months and notes as to whether any special treatment is necessary. As might be expected any species from the high mountains usually needs a period of chilling before it will germinate and on the few occasions where this has not been found to be essential it still does no damage. A number of recondite plants are included in this list, but since anyone interested in such subjects is almost certainly a member of the society I shall not waste space on these. I will summarize most of the genera as follows:

Acaena. *A. adscendens* and *A. anserinifolia* germinate rapidly and well. Other species may take up to three months to germinate and seeds of *A. glabra* show poor germination.

Acantholimon venustum. Germinates poorly and takes up to three months to do so.

Achillea. Neither of the two species described (*A. clavenae* and *A. lingulata*) showed good germination, while in addition, *A. clavenae* took up to three months.

Adonis. Fresh seed appeared to be essential and germinated rapidly.

Aethionema. The most popular species, *A. grandiflorum*, was the least easy with only fair and rather slow germination. Gentle heat was found to be an advantage.

Alyssum. Most species showed good and rapid germination, but the popular *A. saxatile* also needed some heat.

Anacyclus depressus. Showed moderate germination which was not too rapid.

Anagallis. Good and rapid germination.

Androsace. Most species required a period of chilling, which in the case of the most popular and easiest species, *A. lanuginosa* and *A. sarmentosa* required to be followed by a warm treatment. Most were somewhat slow to germinate, but *A. sarmentosa* came up fairly rapidly after its cooling.

Anemone. In many species fresh seed appeared to be essential and germination varied considerably in speed from species to species.

Aquilegia. No cooling was necessary even for the mountain species. In the cases of *AA. alpina, bertolonii*, and *flabellata*, fresh seed appeared to be necessary to get the best results, but even so *A. bertolonii* might prove unsatisfactory, as results seemed very variable. Some heat was necessary for *AA. canadensis, flabellata, pyrenaica* and *saximontana*. Germination was usually fairly rapid, but took from one to three months in the cases of *AA. einseleana, saximontana, scopulorum* and *viridiflora*. Germination was usually good, but for *A. laramiensis* and *A. pyrenaica* was consistently poor, and for *A. scopulorum* was variable, which suggests that here too fresh seed would prove advantageous.

Arabis. No species seemed to require chilling and most germinated well and rapidly.

Arenaria. Here again good germination was found for all species tried except *A. rossii*, but the time of germination varied from one species to the next, although none took longer than three months. No chilling was needed, even for *A. groenlandica*.

Armeria. Generally, there appeared no problems, although germination might be up to three months, but complete failure was recorded with the Spanish *A. caespitosa*.

Arnica. Germinated well and rapidly provided fresh seed was available.

Asclepias. *A. tuberosa*, which is usually regarded as an herbaceous plant, germinated well, but was extremely slow. This would probably be somewhat improved with heat.

Aster. No chilling seemed necessary for the alpine forms, but fresh seed was required for *A. alpinus* and *A. pyrenaeus*, while some heat was necessary for *A. farreri*. Germination was usually good and fairly rapid, but two obscure species showed poor germination.

Astilbe. Chilling was required by *A. chinensis*, but not by *A. simplicifolia*. Germination was good and reasonably rapid.

Astragalus. Only one species was tested and this showed poor germination and took up to three months for the seeds to germinate. With some species soaking the seed for twenty-four hours before sowing has proved helpful with me.

Aubrietia. As one might expect there was good and rapid germination, although the most usually seen, *A. deltoidea* needed gentle heat to get early germination.

Brunnera macrophylla. Tends to have very poor germination, which may take up to three months. (It is like forget-me-not.)

Calandrinia umbellata. Seed needed chilling, after which it germinated rapidly.

Calceolaria. Only the dwarf alpine species were tried and most gave good and rapid germination, although *C. darwinii* could take quite a time and *C. falklandica* was rather slow. Fresh seed was necessary for good results with *C. fothergillii*.

Campanula. As might have been expected we have results for a very large number of species. Generally germination was good and took place rapidly. Chilling was generally not necessary, but appeared to be essential for *CC. lasiocarpa, raineri, waldsteiniana* and *zoysii*. In the case of *C. waldsteiniana*, this chilling had to be followed by gentle heat. Gentle heat was also found to be helpful in the cases of *CC. carpatica*, *formanekiana*, and *garganica*. It was not indicated for *C. fragilis*, which may explain why this seed was apparently rather slow to germinate. Although germination in campanulas was generally good, it was described as *poor* for *CC. cenisia*, *pilosa*, *piperi*, *taurica*, *tridentata* and *versicolor* and only *fair*, for *CC. morettiana*, *patula*, *petiolata*, *poscharskyana*, *rotundifolia* and *tommasiniana*. It must be emphasized that many of these conclusions are drawn from quite a small number of records and it might well have proved different if some of the higher alpines such as *CC. cenisia*, *morettiana* (which apparently germinated very slowly, taking over three months), and *tommasiniana* had been chilled.

Celmisia. Fresh seed of these New Zealand daisies seems to be essential. Even so, as gathered in this country, only a small percentage of the seed germinates, although better results were obtained with *C. coriacea* and *C. spectabilis*. Germination was usually rapid, but *C. angustifolia* took from one to three months and results for *C. coriacea* varied considerably; some sowings germinated rapidly, while others took over a month.

Codonopsis. Varied so much from species to species, both in the germination percentages and in the time taken for the seeds to germinate (although this was never longer than three months) that it seems impossible to make any conclusions. We have already mentioned that at Bressingham Gardens they feel that fresh seed is essential for this genus.

Coprosma. Took about three months to germinate.

Cornus canadensis. Results showed that they took a very long time to germinate. Since the fruit of this is an edible berry, such a result was only to be expected and the seeds probably need similar treatment to those of crataegus and cotoneaster, which will be described in the next section.

Cortusa matthioli. Germinated well and rapidly after chilling.

Cremanthodium. The only species recorded gave good, although rather slow germination, but getting the seeds to germinate is the least of the grower's problems with this genus. In the 1930s, when many of these attractive Himalayan composites were coming into the country, practically no one except Mr. Thomas Hay succeeded in bringing them into flower. He maintained that the seedlings would not tolerate the slightest disturbance of the roots, so he sowed a few seeds in small pots and, after they had germinated, reduced the plants to one per pot. No one has yet come up with a better method and now seeds are again occasionally available, it is as well to be reminded of this.

Cyclamen. Appeared to do best when the seed was fresh and old seed of *C. libanoticum* did not germinate for two years. Even with fresh seed germination was not always very rapid and it is clear one should not give up too rapidly with cyclamen seed.

Delphinium. Of the various species tried, gentle heat was often found helpful in accelerating germination, which varied from rapid for some species, to up to three months with others, while *D. menziesii* took over three months to germinate.

Dianthus. Chilling was only found to be essential for *D. glacialis*, while some heat was found helpful for *DD. arenarius*, *carthusianorum*, *deltoides*, *glacialis* (naturally after the chilling), the hybrid known as 'La Bourbille', *myrtinervius*, *nitidus*, and *superbus*. It might well prove helpful with all species. It seems odd that no chilling was required for *D. alpinus*, as it is usually a high alpine and must get chilling in nature. Generally germination for this genus proved good and rapid, although for *D. glacialis* it was variable.

Dicentras. Usually proved poor germinators. Fresh seed was recommended for *D. peregrina*. Germination varied from three months to longer and for *D. formosa* they recommend chilling, followed by gentle heat.

Digitalis. Often benefited from gentle heat, when they showed good and rapid germination.

Dionysia. Seed required chilling and was usually rather slow to germinate after that.

Dodecatheon. Usually required no chilling, but chilling helped *D. pauciflorum*. They are rather alarming seedlings to raise as all they do is to produce two cotyledons, which enlarge considerably, but die down after about two months so that one thinks the plants are dead. However, they do but rest and come up quite happily the following spring. The mature plants behave in much the same way; coming up in the spring and dying back soon after they have finished flowering. *D. pauciflorum*, although one of the more attractive species, is very slow to germinate and one can rely on having to wait at least three months. The others are not particularly rapid, except for the favourite, *D. meadia*.

Draba. Like most crucifers tends to germinate fairly rapidly. Heat helped *D. aizoides* (which also germinated badly). Chilling without subsequent heat was recommended for *D. hispanica*.

Dryas octopetala. The seed was always very poor, some gatherings containing no live seed at all.

Edraianthus. Gave some interesting results. By and large no chilling was required and gentle heat was appreciated, but exactly the opposite was obtained with *E. kitaibelii* where the seeds needed chilling, but heat appeared to inhibit germination.

Gaultheria. Needed no chilling, but several species germinated more rapidly in gentle heat, although most species took over a month to germinate.

Gentiana. Seemed, as one might have expected, to need a variety of treatments. Chilling was necessary with *GG. acaulis, algida, andrewsii, asclepiadea, dahurica, pannonica, pneumonanthe, punctata, purpurea, septemfida* and *verna*, as well as some rather obscure species. Heat was helpful (sometimes after chilling), with *GG. asclepiadea, dahurica, gelida, gracilipes, lagodechiana, pannonica* and *verna*. Fresh seed usually gave better reults and seemed to be essential for *GG. cruciata, gracilipes* and a couple of rather obscure species, while light was also necessary to secure germination for a number of species (*GG. asclepiadea, cruciata, freyniana, gracilipes, punctata* and *purpurea*). It is probably safe to assume that all gentians benefit from chilling and that all require light to germinate, as the seeds are very minute. Indeed they are so small that it is not easy to stratify them, except by sowing them and putting the pots either outside during winter or in the refrigerator. Even so, in many cases germination is eventually more rapid if they are brought into heat after their chilling. Under these circumstances germination is quite rapid in the majority of cases, although there always seem to be some seeds that may remain for a further year.

Geranium spp. Seemed to be quite straightforward in their germination, although some extra heat in the spring proved beneficial.

Geum. Gave varied results. Chilling was necessary for *G. montanum* but not, rather oddly, for *G. reptans*, which usually grows at a higher elevation in the mountains and germination was never very good in any of the species tried.

Globularia. Was even more confusing. Chilling was found necessary for *GG. cordifolia, incanescens* and *nudicaulis*, and this should be followed by some additional heat, which is appreciated by almost all the genus. The exception is *G. bellidifolia*, which will not germinate at all if the temperature is too high and in any case showed poor germination, which was extremely slow. Most other species gave fairly good and rapid germination.

Haberlea rhodopensis. Needed heat, but even so germination was poor.

Hellebores. It was confirmed that fresh seed is essential.

Heloniopsis. The main secret seemed to be to sow the seed in January, although the seeds might take up to three months to germinate.

Houstonia. Germinated better if given additional heat in spring.

Hypericum. This applied too to some species, and probably all would appreciate the extra heat.

Irises. With their wide distribution they showed a variety of reactions. Chilling appeared necessary for *II. forrestii, pseudacorus* (which takes a long time to germinate), *ruthenica* and *setosa*. Fresh seed was essential to get *I. decora* (syn. *I. nepalensis*) to grow, while cool conditions were essential for *I. tectorum* and placing seeds of this in heat actually prevented germination.

Edelweiss. (*Leontopodium alpinum*.) Behaved like any hardy perennial and gave good germination without any chilling being necessary.

Libertia ixioides. Germinated rapidly in gentle heat.

Lewisia. Somewhat confusing. Only *L. rediviva* appeared to require chilling and it then needed heat afterwards. Heat was also found helpful with *L. cotyledon* and its hybrids. On the other hand too high a temperature stopped the seeds of *L. pygmaea* from germinating. The other species appeared to need no special treatment.

Linum. We have already mentioned the curious fact that chilling was only necessary for the seeds of *L. viscosum*. Heat seemed to help *L. alpinum*, but not any of the other species.

Lobelia. *L. cardinalis* required chilling followed by heat. Chilling was also necessary for *L. linnaeoides*. No special treatment was needed for other species, including *L. syphilitica*, although this latter does germinate more rapidly in heat.

Loiseleuria procumbens. Chilling followed by heat was necessary to get the seeds to germinate. Even so they might take three months.

Lupinus. The alpine species from North America needed the seeds to be soaked in hot water for twelve hours before sowing. This is best done in a thermos flask which keeps the water warm throughout the period. A temperature of around 40° C (104° F) is suitable.

Meconopsis. Oddly enough chilling was not found to be essential, although it had previously been advised for the Himalayan and Sino-Himalayan species. The sole exception was *M. nepalensis*. Heat in spring was recommended for *M. betonicifolia* and *M. regia*. Most of us have found that it is not particularly hard to get meconopsis seed to germinate, but that heavy losses occur when the seedlings are pricked out and it is certainly worth having sterilized loam in your composts at this stage, if you are using a loam-based compost.

Myosotis. Fresh seed was essential for the alpine varieties.

Narcissus triandrus. Fresh seed was found to be necessary. Like all narcissus species it would only germinate after passing the winter outside.

Nomocharis. Very slow to germinate, but finally gave good results. It sounds as though chilling might help here.

Omphalodes luciliae and **Omphalogramma**. Fresh seed was essential.

Oxytropis uralensis. Needed chilling followed by heat, but even so results were not good. Possibly the seeds should be soaked separately before sowing, to ensure that they have absorbed water.

Penstemon. Dwarf penstemons from North America all germinated well in spring in gentle heat.

Phyteuma. Chilling followed by heat is recommended for *P. comosum* and chilling without subsequent heat for *P. scheuzeri* and *P. sieberi*. Other species seemed to need no particular treatment.

Potentilla. In this species chilling was only found necessary for *P. nevadensis*. Heat helped the germination of *P. aurea* and *P. eriocarpa*. Germination was usually good and rapid, but the seeds of *P. nitida* gave very poor germination and the seeds of *P. eriocarpa* were nothing special.

Primula. By far the most complete results come from this genus. It should be borne in mind that generally we are considering seeds sown in the spring, at any time from February to April. In very many cases light was found to be essential for germination and it can probably be given safely in all cases. This means that the seeds are either sown on the surface or very lightly covered. It appears to be mainly the infra-red light that seeds require and this can, apparently, pierce a very light covering. However, there were cases where fresh seed appeared essential, and so spring sowing would not be feasible. This was found with *P. auricula* and the garden auriculas. It is true that here one can often get some results from seed that is not fresh, but germination is then extremely unreliable. Fresh seed was also essential for *PP. edgeworthii, gaubeana, nutans* and *reidii*. It is also said to be necessary for *P. sonchifolia* and probably others of the Petiolaris section. We have already noted how some of these shed their seeds while they are still green and that they after-ripen in the soil. Chilling was found to be necessary in the following species: *PP. calderiana, capitellata, chungensis, clusiana, cynoglossifolia, darialica, glaucescens, integrifolia, ioessa,* *iaponica*, *macrophylla*, *marginata*, *minima*, *mollis*, *nivalis*, *rubra*, *sherriffae*, *spectabilis*, *stricta* and *viscosa*. Some heat was found to speed up germination in the cases of *PP*. *beesiana*, *calderiana*, *farinosa*, *pulverulenta*, *secundiflora*, *vialii* and *waltonii*. When the various species were given the appropriate treatment, germination was usually fairly rapid, although more than a month might elapse before seedlings were seen; plants that took a long time to germinate (over three months) were *PP*. *capitellata*, *integrifolia*, *rubra* and *specuicola*. It may be assumed that any species which does not figure in this list (provided that it is not a very obscure and little-grown species), needs no special treatment of any sort.

Ptilotrichum spinosum. Germinated better in heat.

Pulsatilla. Fresh seed is essential for all the species and heat helps the germination of *P. vulgaris* and its allies.

Ramonda. Heat is recommended for *R. myconii* (*syn. R. pyrenaica*), but not apparently for *R. nathaliae*, which seems strange as the Balkans are usually warmer than the Pyrenees.

Rhododendron. Fresh seed is said to be essential for *R. camtschaticum* and chilling for *R. ferrugineum*.

Saussurea discolor. This odd woolly Himalayan composite is said to require chilling followed by heat.

Saxifraga. Most seeds need the chilling treatment; the exceptions being the Robinsonia section (London pride and the like), and *S. granulata* and its allies. Presumably it would not be necessary for the Spanish species, *S. boissieri* and the like, which do not appear to have been studied. It seems to be necessary for most of the others, particularly the Aizoons and the Kabaschias. Fresh seed is advised for *S. longifolia*. In the case of *S. hostii* we are advised to sow outdoors in February. Heat is recommended for *S. moschata* and *S. rosacea* after the chilling process has been completed. Germination is very slow in the cases of most of the encrusted saxifragas, although *S. longifolia* germinated rapidly from fresh seed. But in most cases germination might take three months.

Scabious. Fresh seed generally gave the best results. Too much heat prevented the seed of *S. lucida* from germinating.

Scutellaria. Two species were tested with completely opposing results. Fresh seed of *S. alpina* germinated well and rapidly, while seed of *S. laterifolia* required chilling and was extremely slow to germinate after this process was completed.

Sedum. Gave rather mixed results. Chilling was necessary only for *S. populifolium*, but some heat was helpful both for this species and for *S. spathulifolium*, while complete failure was experienced with *S. cauticola*.

Senecio greyi. Seed germinated poorly and very slowly. Since the plant grown commercially under this name is probably a hybrid, it may well be that many seeds do not develop properly.

Silene. A large number of species were tested and for the majority no special treatment appeared necessary. However, chilling was found necessary in the cases of *SS. acaulis, flavescens* and *ingramii*; while some heat was helpful with *SS. armeria, flavescens* and *schafta*. Germination was usually good and fairly rapid, but very slow in the case of *S. ingramii* and very poor for *S. delavayi*.

Soldanella. Fresh seed was essential for *S. alpina* and *S. carpatica*, but in the case of *S. montana*, chilling was found necessary. All species germinated well, but took from one to three months to do so.

Talinum. Most species benefited from some heat.

Townsendia. Benefited from some heat, but *T. hookeri* needed preliminary chilling, but this was unnecessary for *T. exscapa*.

Trollius. The only species tested, *T. pumilis*, required chilling followed by heat and it seems reasonable to suppose that chilling would be required by all species of this genus.

Vaccinium. Almost all species required chilling followed by heat. However, chilling was found unnecessary for *V. arctostaphylos*, while heat actually prevented the seed of *V. ovatum* from germinating.

Veronica. Among the various species tested, chilling was found necessary for *V. fruticans* and heat helped the germination of *V. gentianoides*, otherwise they presented no problem. *V. fruticans* was also very slow to germinate.

It must be borne in mind that some of these results were only obtained after a single sowing, so that some of the results may need to be modified subsequently. Even so it must be regarded as an extremely useful list of findings and one wishes that it could have been repeated in other types of plant.

Woody plants

In point of fact we do have quite a bit of information about the behaviour of many trees and shrubs. This is all summarized in W. G. Sheat's *Propagation of Trees, Shrubs and Conifers*, now out of print. This book is intended for the commercial nurseryman, rather than for the amateur grower, so some of the techniques suggested have been modified by me.

Acer. Many of the maples and sycamores have rather moist seeds and may lose their vitality if allowed to become too dry. For most species seed is best collected, the wings broken off and sown as soon as ripe. The seed is usually left out of doors, but some protection against mice and other vermin is necessary. Most species germinate the following spring. However, *AA. campestre, monspessulanum* and *opalus* require a year's stratification and only germinate the second spring after gathering. The viability of acer seeds varies considerably. Almost every seed of the sycamore or the Norway maple will germinate, while if you get a 5 per cent germination with *A. griseum*, you may congratulate yourself. With purchased seed there is always a risk that the seeds may have dried out too much, the silver maple, *A. dasycarpum* (syn. *A. saccharinum*) being especially susceptible. It is therefore best to get seeds from friends and neighbours if that is possible.

Aesculus. The seeds of these are very watery and should not be allowed to dry out. So they are best sown as soon as ripe, being buried at least 1 cm ($\frac{1}{2}$ in) deep and either left out of doors or brought into gentle heat after the winter. Here again you must guard against mice and squirrels.

Alnus. In this case the seeds are gathered in the autumn, carefully dried and stored over winter. They are sown in the early spring, and must either be left on the surface or only very lightly covered, as light is necessary for germination.

Amelanchier. This is the first of a series of rosaceous plants, which it is normally necessary to stratify for eighteen months before germination can be expected. As we have seen this is due to the necessity for first a cooling period and secondly for the impermeable seed coat to be softened, so that the seed can imbibe water. In nature, passing through a bird or mammal's digestive tract seems to effect this, so that such seeds may well germinate in the following spring. It is possible that filing the seeds or rubbing them with glass paper, so as to remove a small portion of this hard coat, might equally expedite matters. This would be a delicate matter with small seeds such as those of amelanchier, but would be easier with seeds of crataegus and similar fruits, which also otherwise need this long period of stratification. The technique would at least be worth trying. It is not often that the amateur requires many plants of any of these species, so it would not be necessary to operate on very many seeds. I am by no means sure that this always works, but I have had some success with crataegus species. Otherwise with amelanchier the recommended technique is to gather the seed as soon as ripe, usually early July, remove the seeds from the surrounding pulp, mix with moist sand and keep in this condition out of doors until the second spring. Germination is then generally rapid and good.

Arbutus. If imported seed of the madrona, *A. menziesii* is obtained, it has to be soaked for five to six days in warm water before being sown in the spring. The only way to keep the water consistently warm is to use a thermos flask, although even so it is best to change the water each day. Where fresh fruits of the various species are available, it is only necessary to separate the seed from the pulp as much as possible and sow immediately.

Aronia. The seed needs chilling either by being sown and left outdoors during the winter, or by being mixed with moist sand and put in the refrigerator for twelve weeks. It is usually sown in March.

Berberis. If you are gathering seed, collect it as soon as the fruit is ripe. Apparently the longer it is left on the bushes, the less viable it becomes. The seed should be removed from the pulp and mixed with moist sand and stratified over winter. Sowing should take place early in February and germination will naturally be expedited if gentle heat can be given at this time. If you are obtaining seed from a garden where many species are grown, there is a grave risk that the seed may not come true to the species. Still, often the chance hybrids may be very pleasant plants. The handsomely fruited *B.* x *rubrostilla* was the result of one such unintentional hybrid. Usually the seed germinates rapidly and well.

Betula. Birches should have the seed gathered as soon as it is ripe. This can be observed when the catkins start to disintegrate. It seems best for the seed to be sown immediately, but quite good results have been obtained from gathering the seed when ripe and storing in a dry cool place until early spring. The birches from northern Europe and North America need at least sixteen hours of daylight, before they germinate, which in practice means that this takes place generally in June. The Indian and Chinese species germinate with less length of daylight. Birch seed should never be covered, but pressed on to the surface of the soil. If the seed is stored, it should still be sown about February, even though it will be some time before germination actually takes place.

Buddleia. There seems to be some rather inconclusive evidence that buddleia seed germinates best in darkness, so it is recommended to cover the container with paper until germination occurs.

Camellia. Seed is not usually much used with these shrubs, but it is perfectly feasible for species or if you should wish to sow the seed of hybrids to see if any good plants might result. However, it is not particularly easy to get camellia seeds to germinate and fresh seeds should be obtained when possible. These should be soaked in warm water for twenty-four hours.

They are then dried and lightly filed around the place where the seed was attached to the ovary. The seed coat should not be cut through, but should be reduced. The seed is then sown with the filed portion facing downwards and the seeds covered by 6 mm ($\frac{1}{4}$ in) of soil in some heat. Under these circumstances we are told that germination is rapid.

Caragana. Like many members of the pea family some preliminary soaking of the seed before sowing is helpful. For this genus about three hours in warm water is all that is necessary.

Carpinus. Seeds of the hornbeam should be sown in the autumn as soon as they are ripe. As with the maples, the wings are broken off the seeds before sowing. The seeds are left outside all the winter and most will germinate in the spring. However, germination of hornbeams may well be irregular, with some of the seeds remaining in the soil until the following spring.

Carya. We are always told that the only satisfactory way to get good hickory trees is to grow them from seed, so that they can be planted out with the tap-root undamaged. Unfortunately this seems to be a counsel of perfection, as the seeds are never available. If, however, you have some private correspondence with growers in the U.S.A., and can obtain hickory nuts in the autumn, they should be put in moist sand and kept in it over the winter. In February sow the seeds singly in the extra long pots known as 'long toms'. Germination seems to take place best under fairly cool conditions, but the plants can be brought into warmth as soon as germination has occurred. When sufficiently advanced harden the seedlings off and place them in their permanent positions as soon as all risk of spring frosts is past, usually early June. You should never attempt to crack the nuts to extract the kernel and they should be well buried in the pots.

Castanea. Sweet chestnut seeds should be gathered as soon as ripe and kept in moist peat until late January, when they can be sown, 5 cm (2 in) deep in the open ground. Germination takes place in the spring, but this early sowing seems to be essential. Presumably they could be sown in the autumn, but mice and squirrels would be hard to control at this stage and they are still a danger with the late January sowing.

Chaenomeles. One would have expected the seed of the japonicas to have needed some chilling, but this is apparently not so. Sheat recommends gathering the seed and drying it in the autumn and sowing under glass in February.

Cotoneaster. The seed should be gathered as soon as ripe, mixed with moist sand and either left in the refrigerator or put in a polythene bag which is buried in a pot outside. In late February take the sand and the seeds and rub them thoroughly through your hands. Apparently this is sufficient to abrade the hard seed coats, but it is clear that very gritty sand must be used. The seed is buried about 1 cm deep and should germinate rapidly and evenly. The very late ripening species such as *CC. glaucophyllus, serotinus* and *lacteus* may wait until the following spring before they germinate, but this is not invariable and you may get germination the same spring as those species which ripen their fruits earlier.

Crataegus. The seeds have extremely hard coats and normally require a warm period to make them permeable and a chilling period to break dormancy, so that they are usually stratified for eighteen months. However, the treatment suggested for amelanchier, p. 89, may also work here and the seeds are large enough to handle with ease. Sheat recommends a rather richer compost for these seeds, which should be buried 1 cm. The compost is three parts sterilized loam, one part peat and one part sharp sand. It seems probable that JIP 1 would prove satisfactory for these. Although the initial progress is rather slow, once established, crataegus make much more rapid growth than purchased plants and may well flower after six years.

Cytisus. Soaking the seed for twenty-four hours before sowing seems beneficial.

Daphne. The seeds should be gathered as soon as ripe, removed from the pulp and mixed with only slightly moist sand until the spring. No harm can follow from rubbing the seed and sand through your hands before sowing, but it does not appear to be essential. The seeds usually germinate with unusual ease for the seed of drupes.

Davidia. The large nuts of the handkerchief tree should be gathered in October and stratified in moist sand. In late February they should be removed from the sand and buried in boxes of moist peat and put in gentle heat. As soon as a nut germinates it should be potted up singly either in JIP 1 or in the proposed crataegus compost. Germination is usually good and rapid, once the stratification is complete.

Diospyros. The seed of persimmon and its allies should be gathered when ripe and removed from the pulp. It is stratified in moist sand over winter and sown in gentle heat in March. Sheat recommends a compost of two parts moss peat and one part sharp sand.

Elaeagnus. Seed of this needs the same treatment as crataegus with stratification for eighteen months. Since seed is not easy to come by and the plants are easily raised from layers or cuttings, this is not often done.

Euonymus. The seed is gathered as soon as ripe and stored in *dry* sand until the spring. No chilling appears to be necessary, but dry sand is necessary to prevent excessive desiccation. The seeds are then sown in spring as though no special treatment had been required.

Exochorda. Here, again, it is necessary to gather the seed as soon as ripe and store in dry sand until the seed is sown in February or March.

Fagus. The seed is gathered when ripe and stored in moist peat until the spring or, alternatively, it can be sown in the autumn, but in that case precautions against vermin must be taken. If stored in moist peat, the seed is removed and sown in the ordinary way in the spring.

Fraxinus. The seed is sown in the autumn as soon as it is ripe. The wings are removed from the keys, although this is only to give ease of handling and the seeds are buried 6 mm ($\frac{1}{4}$ in) deep. If left outdoors, the seed starts to germinate very early in the spring and the seedlings need protection from frost.

Fremontodendron. The seeds need soaking for forty-eight hours in lukewarm water before sowing. This will entail the use of a thermos flask. The seeds are then sown singly in thumb pots either in JIP 1 or in the crataegus compost, covered only very lightly and well watered in. Some heat is necessary for germination, so if this cannot be supplied in March, it is as well to delay sowing until the natural temperature is fairly high; 25° C (77° F) is a good daytime reading.

Gaultheria. This gets an entry here only because one might assume that a berry-like seed would require special treatment. On the contrary, after removing the pulp, the seed is dried and stored in a dry place until it is sown in early spring.

Gleditsia. Soaking the seed in very hot water for an hour before sowing seems to be sufficient. The seeds can either be sown one to a pot or thinly in boxes. They are covered about 1 cm.

Gymnocladus. No especial treatment seems to be necessary to secure some germination, but this may well be improved by soaking the seeds in absolute alcohol for twenty-four hours.

Halesia. Seeds of the snowdrop tree are gathered as soon as ripe and stratified over winter in moist peat. They are sown in early March, the seeds being buried about 1 cm.

Hippophae. Seeds of the sea buckthorn are stored in *dry* sand over winter. The berries are usually ripe in October. The seeds are sown in spring with only a very light covering. Under these circumstances germination is quick and good.

Ilex. Here we have another seed with a very hard coat, which presumably gets more permeable after passing through birds or mice. Without this it seems necessary to stratify the seeds in *dry* sand for at least eighteen months. Germination can usually be expected in the second spring after gathering. Whether a year could be saved by filing the seed coats with glass paper or some other abrasive may well be worth an experiment. Hollies are rather slow growers under all circumstances and it is only commercial establishments which are likely to raise hollies in this way, as stocks for the various cultivars.

Juniperus. Most conifers show fairly rapid germination, once they have ripened their seed, but junipers behave as though they were fruits of the rose family and require stratifying in a mixture of moist peat and sand for eighteen months. Rubbing the seed through sharp sand so as to scarify the seed coat, will cause some seeds to germinate more rapidly, but in this case germination is uneven, whereas, if you stratify for eighteen months, all the seeds will germinate together.

Juglans. The main problem in growing walnuts from seed occurs during the winter. Once ripe the seed is stored in boxes of barely moist peat. If the peat is too damp, there is a risk of the seeds falling victim to mildew, while if it is too dry the seed can be killed. It is therefore advisable to examine the peat frequently and moisten it very slightly if it becomes dry. The nuts and peat are generally stored in a cool dry shed and both these conditions are necessary. The seeds are sown in the usual compost in the spring, buried about 2·5 cm (1 in) below the surface, when good germination may be expected.

Lagerstroemia. If fresh seed is obtainable for this rather tender shrub, it is best sown as soon as ripe in late autumn. A heated greenhouse (or a window sill in a centrally-heated house) will be necessary to bring the seedlings up and through the winter. With old seed, germination is very irregular.

Leycesteria. The seed must be freed of pulp when ripe, which is usually by late October. It can then either be stratified in sand until the spring, or taken and rubbed through the hands with gritty sand and sown at once in gentle heat. The seed should be lightly buried about 6 mm ($\frac{1}{4}$ in).

Magnolia. If fresh seed is available, germination is usually good, although the time taken is variable. If it is not available germination is very doubtful. With small quantities the simplest method is to sow the seed as soon as gathered and leave outside over winter. The seeds are quite deeply buried, up to 2·5 cm (1 in). If for some reason this is not suitable, the seeds can be stratified in *dry* sand over winter. In February the seed is removed from the dry sand and mixed with moist sand and left for about a fortnight. The seed is then removed and washed in water and then sown in gentle heat. The stratification seems particularly suitable for the North American species. Generally if either of these methods are pursued, germination is good and rapid, but there are stories of some species, particularly *M. wilsonii*, taking three years to germinate. Purchased seed should be sown as soon as received, but even so its success is doubtful and long delays may well be necessary. Many forms of the popular *M.* x *soulangiana* do not set seed, but the cultivar known as 'Lennei' does; the seedlings will usually differ from the parent to a greater or lesser degree.

Malus. See **Pyrus.**

Mespilus. Medlars are tiresome to grow from seed. Get the fruit and lay them out in the open until they start to decay. Then remove the seeds and stratify in a mixture of moist peat and sand for about fifteen months, sowing the seed in the second spring after gathering.

Myrica. It seems to be essential to sow the seed as soon as it is ripe. It is lightly covered and overwintered either outside or in a cold frame. The containers are brought in to gentle heat at the end of February; good germination is usually obtained.

Ostrya. The hop hornbeam tends to germinate somewhat irregularly whatever treatment is given, but the recommended method is to stratify the seed over winter in a mixture of equal parts of moist peat and sand, and sow the seeds either outdoors or in gentle heat in the spring. Most seeds will probably germinate in the first spring, but some will not do so until the following season.

Paliurus. Although there is no connection between the two genera, these spiny plants need the same treatment for their seeds as recommended for myrica: immediate sowing, overwintering in a cold frame and being brought into gentle heat about February. Germination is moderate.

Pernettya. Here again the treatment is the same as that for gaultheria. The seeds are removed as soon as the berries are ripe, cleaned of pulp, dried and stored in bags until the spring.

Phellodendron. Purchased seed needs no special treatment, but fresh seed is gathered in the autumn, cleaned of the gummy substance which surrounds the seeds and stored in dry sand until the spring.

Photinia. The treatment here is the same as that for cotoneaster. The seed is stratified in moist sand over winter. In the spring the seed and sand are rubbed by the hands sufficiently to scarify the seed coats slightly. The seed is buried about 1 cm and germination is usually free.

Pinus. There is usually no trouble in getting the seeds to germinate, but some species are remarkably disinclined to open their cones. Incidentally, all pine cones take two years for the seeds to ripen. If after this time the cones have not opened and you want seed, the simplest method is to put the seeds in a very low oven until they do open. Often in the wild it needs a forest fire to open the cones, so the seeds will tolerate unusually high temperatures. Even so the oven should not be hotter than 200° F (around 94° C). Once the cones are open, the seeds are sown in spring in the ordinary way.

Pistacia. The berries are soaked in alkaline water, that is water in which a little lime or washing soda has been dissolved, for sixteen hours. The seeds are then removed from the pulp by mixing with grit and rubbing through the hands until the seeds are clear of all pulp. The seeds are sown thinly in gentle heat in spring, buried about 1 cm, or slightly less.

Pyrus. The method applies also to malus and sorbus,* and more or less to prunus and is simplicity itself. The seeds are sown as soon as ripe and the containers left out of doors throughout the winter. Most of the seeds will germinate in the spring and this may be helped if they are brought into gentle heat in March. However, there are always some seeds which will take two seasons to germinate, so if you do not get enough plants in the first spring, it is worth while keeping the containers going until the following spring. Most amateurs do not require large numbers of trees and shrubs, although they are, of course, useful for swapping with other gardeners.

Quercus. Since oaks are very slow growing, they are probably not the first choice among those who wish to raise trees

* But see page 100.

from seed, but they are fascinating. The acorns should be gathered as soon as they are ripe. This is usually at the end of the first autumn, but in some species it takes two years for the acorns to ripen and it is worth while finding out which these are. Among the species most frequently met with which have this characteristic are *QQ. coccinea*, x *hispanica*, *palustris* and *rubra*.

Acorns of the North American white oaks, of which *Q. bicolor* is the only one that is at all satisfactory in Great Britain, require sowing at once, as they start to produce roots immediately, although no shoots are seen until the spring. Other species are stratified over winter in moist peat and sand, although, provided they are kept clear of vermin, there is no reason why they too should not be sown in autumn and left outdoors. If they are stratified, they are sown in the spring either outdoors or in gentle heat. All acorns are buried at least 1 cm beneath the surface and slightly greater depths do not appear to do any harm. The only real trouble in raising oaks is preserving the acorns from pests; this operation must be continued for the second season as the acorns have a large food reserve on which the young plant depends for over twelve months.

Raphiolepis. The seed does not usually mature until the autumn, when it must be sown at once in a heated greenhouse. Imported seed is sown in spring, but does not germinate so well and even with fresh seed germination is not particularly good.

Rhododendron. We have already mentioned the recommended seed compost, but it should, perhaps, be repeated here. Coarse lumpy peat is put at the bottom of the container, topped by a 1 cm ($\frac{1}{2}$ in) layer of equal parts of loam, sharp sand and peat, the container is then topped up with sifted moss peat. Water well in and then add a thin layer of very finely sifted moss peat. The seed, which is very fine, should be sown as thinly as possible and just pressed in on the surface; light seems to be necessary for germination. It is as well to place a sheet of glass over the container, unless the sandwich box technique mentioned on page (35) is used, as one does not want to water the seedlings more than is essential. Provided the seeds have been sown sufficiently thinly they can be left in their containers for more than a year; indeed until they are large enough to handle. The main danger to seedlings would seem to be the arrival of moss, which can smother the tiny plantlets, so a close watch must be kept and any sign of moss should be at once removed. Although rhododendron and azalea seeds are so dust-like and the plants seem to grow so slowly for the first two years, a surprising number will flower in the fifth year from sowing. When you compare the price of rhododendrons with a packet of seed you will appreciate how worth while it is to undertake this operation. In their second or third year the seedlings are usually pricked out in boxes and transferred to the open ground either in their third or their fourth year, depending on the size.

The tiny seedlings should always be in a shady situation as burning sun can quickly scorch them up, even though the compost may be moist. This compost must never be allowed to dry out at any time, as the seedlings have little root and all rhododendrons are rather susceptible to dry conditions and can easily perish from drought, even when mature.

Rosa. The seed is gathered when the heps are ripe, removed and washed and then stratified in moist sand until the spring. Most will then germinate, but it is occasionally necessary to wait until the second spring.

Rubus. Seed is not often used for this genus, as vegetative methods of increase are so easy. If, however, it is attempted the berries should be gathered and rubbed through the hands with sharp sand, dried and stored until spring, when they are sown in the usual way.

Sambucus. Elders can be treated in the same way as rubus, but it is usually sufficient to remove the seeds from the pulp, dry, and sow in spring.

Salix. The seed is said to be very short-lived and must be sown as soon as it is ripe, which can be recognized when it starts to blow away from the catkins. It is not very often that people worry about raising willows from seed as hardwood cuttings root so very easily.

Skimmia. This is yet another case where eighteen months' stratification in moist sand is recommended, after removing the seeds from the pulp. It would also seem to be a case where scarifying the seed coats might speed up germination.

Sophora. The seeds are sown in spring in the usual way, but germination is said to be speeded up by soaking the seeds for two hours in very hot water. This necessitates a thermos flask. Sheat recommends a rather sandy compost made up of two parts sand to one part each of peat and loam.

Sorbus. This has always proved rather unsatisfactory from seed. The usual process was to sow the seed in the autumn, let it winter outside and bring into the warm, as soon as germination was observed. A few seedlings would appear and possibly more the second spring but, even so, the percentage of germination was poor. Recent research at the Kinsealy Agricultural Research Institute suggests that better results may be obtained by first subjecting the seed to a very warm period: three months at 25° C (77° F) followed by three months at 0–2° C (32–36° F). This is evidently not easy for amateurs, but it would perhaps give satisfactory results if the pot of seed were put in the airing cupboard and then in the freezing compartment of a refrigerator.

Stranvaesia. The seed is ripe in late October, when it should be gathered and mixed with moist sand to be stratified over winter. It is then sown in the spring, when germination is usually good and rapid. The seed should be buried about 6 mm ($\frac{1}{4}$ in).

Symphoricarpos. It is as well that the snowberries come readily from cuttings, as the seeds require eighteen months' stratification; the actual seeds are too small to permit of scarification, so a prolonged warm period is necessary before the seed coat will become permeable to water.

Taxus. Yews are yet another case of either an eighteen-month stratification being necessary or else scarification followed by chilling.

Tilia. If fresh lime seed is available, it should be stratified in moist sand over winter and not sown until early April. Seed that is not fresh should be sown when received—and then hope for the best. The seed of *T. americana* appears to need eighteen months' stratification. Sheat recommends the same compost as for sophora.

Otherwise it may be assumed that the seed of other shrubs will require no special treatment, but can be gathered when ripe, stored in a dry, cool situation and sown in the spring. It should be perhaps noted that not everyone would agree with all the above treatments and some would recommend eighteen months' stratification for cotoneaster and halesia. With cotoneaster it would seem to depend on how much scarifying takes place when the sand and seed are rubbed through the hands.

Greenhouse plants

There would seem to be singularly little information as to any special treatments required by greenhouse plants. It is fairly clear that normally chilling would not be a suitable treatment for tropical or subtropical seeds, although it might prove to be advantageous for plants from tropical uplands, such as the giant senecios and lobelias from the high African mountains. Since these have proved to be impossible to cultivate in our greenhouses, owing to the fantastic variations in temperature that they experience in the wild, the matter is only of theoretical interest.

Normally, indeed, it would seem that the usual technique of sowing in spring in a rather high temperature will satisfy most of the inhabitants of our greenhouses, but some difficulty is experienced with plants that, like our temperate hawthorns, have berry-like fruits, which are normally eaten by birds or small mammals. Plants like ardisia and rivina often take a long time for the seeds to germinate. The seeds of ardisia are large enough to scarify the seed coats and this might be expected to speed up germination. The seeds of rivina are quite small and it would probably be necessary to try the technique of mixing the seed with fine grit and rubbing vigorously through the hands to make the seed coats permeable.

Many of the *Leguminosae* are renowned for having very hard, impermeable coats and the technique recommended for starting the seeds of wattles (acacia species) into growth is quite outstanding. The seeds are put in a sieve, which is passed to and fro above the flames of burning paper until a seed explodes. When this happens, tip the rest of the seeds into lukewarm water and leave for about thirty minutes. The seeds are then sown and germination is said to be very rapid. In Australia the wattles come up in considerable numbers after forest fires, so this great heat is obviously a good trigger with difficult species. However, many of the better-known species, such as the mimosa and the attractively-leaved *Acacia baileyi* seem to germinate quite well after just a few hours' soaking in warm water.

For some of the species of cassia it has been found that if the seeds are soaked in absolute ethyl alcohol for seventy-two hours, the seed coats become permeable to water and this seems to apply to all the *Caesalpiniae* and the same treatment can be used for caesalpinia and bauhinia.

Cannas have large, very hard seeds. Indeed the first species known in Europe, the West Indian *Canna indica* was known commonly as Indian shot. Most growers file through part of the seed coat before sowing, although others maintain that a twenty-four hours' soak in hot water before sowing is sufficient. Since the first roots are very brittle, the seeds are usually sown singly in small pots and subsequently potted on when necessary. This means that they are treated much the same as hardy bulbs and the compost used is either JIP 1 or its loamless equivalent.

This covers all the special treatments I have been able to gather about greenhouse subjects, but I am doubtful if that is all that we should know and it would be very helpful if gardeners in the tropics and subtropics would share their knowledge with us.

This has been rather a lengthy chapter and may have left you with the thought that seed sowing is an unnecessarily complicated business, but if you think that out of the thousands of plants that we grow in our gardens only a comparatively small number require these special treatments, I hope that this chapter will fall into its rightful perspective.

7 Gathering seed; how to get unusual seeds

Even though you may have enough plants in your garden, there are liable to be many others who will be only too happy to have seeds of many of the plants you grow. Moreover, if you belong to one of the gardening societies that issue a seed list—a point we shall be coming to later in the chapter—you may well find that people who give seeds have a larger choice than those who do not, so it is worth your while to collect seeds of any interesting plants that you have in your garden. You might think it was easy enough to do this, but there are often unexpected problems. For example the seeds of geraniums (and I mean geraniums not pelargoniums) are flung away from the plants as soon as they are ripe and are then undiscoverable, and there are more plants than you would think that have a fairly explosive dispersal system. Such seeds have to be gathered before they are completely ripe.

Indeed most seeds are harvested before they are completely ripe, and, if they have a little portion of stem attached, they will easily ripen even when detached from the plant. The trick, which can really only be learned by experience, is to know when to take the capsules. (The capsule is the name given to the organ which contains the seeds, such as a pod.) However, there are a few general principles, which are more usually correct than not. The majority of capsules, as they ripen, change both in colour and texture. They turn brown or black and instead of being fleshy become dry and brittle. At the same time the ovules, or immature seeds inside, also change colour and become much drier. If you have plenty of capsules it is easy enough to open one, so that, first, you can see if the texture of the capsule is dry and brittle and, secondly, you can see if the contents look like seeds, turning brown or black and do not look particularly plump. If such is the case you can gather all the capsules that look ripe, put them in a paper bag and hang them up in a warm dry place. Usually any room in the house is suitable, so is a dry potting shed, so, indeed, is the airing cupboard.

It is as well to put a label or a piece of paper with the name of the plant written on it with the capsules, so that you know what seed is in that particular bag. Very few plants ripen all their seeds at once, so you will probably have to make several gatherings, before you have got all the seeds of any particular plant. There are, however, some plants which carry their fruits in a spreading panicle, or in an umbel, like the polyanthus, or in a corymb and in these forms all the flowers tend to come out together and therefore all the seeds tend to ripen more or less at the same time. With plants like these you can cut the whole stem when you notice that the capsules are looking ripe and hang them all upside down in your bag, when they will complete their ripening and may well shed their seeds in the bottom of the bag. These are the easiest of seeds to gather.

Another easy seed to get is the peony, for all you have to do here is to watch the seed pods. When they are ripe they split open and the seeds remain in the open pods exposed to the air. Very often you can see some seeds that are red and some that are blue-black. It is only these blue-black ones that are any good. The red ones, that make the open seed pod look so ornamental, have not been fertilized and will never produce a plant. All, therefore, you have to do to collect peony seeds is to wait for the capsules to open (usually in September or October, but sometimes as early as August), and then go round and pick off all the seeds that are black or blue-black. The gladwyn, *Iris foetidissima*, is mainly grown for its ornamental seeds, which are bright red, and they too remain in the open capsules for some time and present no problems. The same cannot be said of all irises, but the capsule splits slightly at the top when the seeds are nearly ripe and they can then be gathered and left to complete their ripening in the paper bags. Incidentally, the bags should be either paper or some similar material; plastic bags are not suitable as the seeds never dry out properly in them.

Trouble starts when the capsules remain green. The worst is the hellebore. With these the petal-like sepals (known as tepals) do not fade and fall off as most petals do and the capsules are hidden from view by them. The flowers hang down, the capsules open at the tips and the seed can be shed before you are aware that they are anywhere near ripe. It is usually late May when the seeds ripen and it is a good idea when you reach this time of year to open a capsule and look inside. If the seeds are brown or black that is the time to collect the capsules; it is probably safe to collect the whole inflorescence with quite a long stem and invert it in your bag. The capsules will open when they are ready and the seed will be found at the bottom of the bag. If you want to grow more hellebores yourself it is as well to sow them right away. You will find some germinate almost at once, while others will wait until the following spring, but if you do not sow them promptly you may well find they take two years to germinate. If, when you looked in the capsules the seeds were white or green, you must wait a week or so and then look again.

The genus *Viola*, the pansies and violets, also keep their capsules green. Eventually these capsules split into three sections, with the seeds lying inside as though they were in a little boat. If you catch them the moment they open you may save the seed, but it is shed very shortly after and it is best to gather the capsules just before they are going to open. This is easier said than done, but you usually have plenty to play with, so it is possible to open a capsule and see if the seeds inside have started to change colour. If they have it is probably safe to gather them and leave them to complete their ripening apart from the plant. Sometimes you can tell by shaking the capsule; if you hear the seeds rattling, then it is safe to gather the capsules. Many of the early flowering violets fail to ripen any seed at all and so they produce a second crop of flowers in June which do make capsules. These flowers have no petals and never open—they are called cleistogamous—but they do produce perfectly good seed, which is usually ready in late June of July. Since this is not a time of the year when you are thinking about violets it is a good idea to write down some reminder if you want violet seed.

Delphiniums and larkspurs often have quite ripe seed while the capsules are still green. They split at the tips, like the hellebores, but fortunately the capsules are not pointing down and it is often possible to rescue the seed even after the capsules have opened. Presumably in nature they are shaken out by the wind. Even so when you do see the bottom capsules in a spike of delphinium or larkspur open, it is as well to gather the nearest unopened ones at the same time.

As far as I am concerned the hardest seeds of all to gather are those from plants belonging to the sage family, *Labiatae*, and to the borage family, *Boraginaceae*. Most of the plants from these families have no seed capsules at all. The seeds form at the base of the sepals, which are long enough to protect them from the weather and when they are ripe they fall out. The only way you can get the seeds is to inspect the plants at regular intervals and see if the seeds are nearly ripe; if they are you must detach the part containing the seed and pop it into your bag. If the plant has a very short spike it may be possible to take the whole spike, but in this case you do not turn it upside down in your bag but keep it in the same position as it was when growing and wait for the seeds to fall out. Unfortunately, the seeds seem to ripen very quickly, so that you look one day and they are not ready and then next time you look they have all been shed. The borage family sometimes do have capsules which makes life easier, but labiates are very tiresome. Since the seeds fall straight down, it is possible to put some white paper, weighed down with pebbles at the base of the stems and collect the seed in this way, but it is never easy. Some plants, such as lavender, do not have the sepals pointing downward and here it is possible to collect the spikes and hang them upside down in the usual way. It is plants like sages and the bastard balm, *Melittis melissophyllum*, which are really difficult.

Even worse, perhaps, are the rhizomatous anemones and many buttercups (ranunculus species) in which the seeds never change colour. If you have the right soil in your garden you may well find self-sown seedlings of *Anemone blanda* coming up everywhere, but you will look in vain for seeds. This is because the little bundle of green achenes in the centre of the flower never change colour at all. If you touch them after the flowers have faded you may find that the little green seeds fall off as soon as you touch them. This is a sign that they are ripe, but you want to catch them before they reach this condition, so when you find a plant in which the achenes do fall off at a touch, it is a good time to collect the other little groups and pop them in a bag. Many people sow them at once, although they do not come up until the next spring, but they may do their after-ripening quite happily in the bag. The same applies to many of the buttercup type ranunculus and other herbaceous and rhizomatous anemones. Such plants as *Ranunculus amplexifolius*, *R. acontifolius* and *R. gouanii* or anemones *blanda*, *apennina*, *nemorosa*, *ranunculoides*, *narcissiflora*, *sylvestris*, *patula* and indeed most species, apart from the tuberous *A. hortensis* and *A. coronaria* which ripen normally, and hepaticas share this tiresome habit. I have been speaking of the achenes as seeds, but strictly speaking the true seeds are inside the green achenes, but they never appear outside the coat of the achene which acts as an additional seed coat.

Care of another kind is required for seeds with some mechanism for throwing the seed some distance from the plant. Geraniums are typical of this group. They are called cranesbills because the seed head, with its long beak, looks much like the head of a long-billed bird. The beak is made up of a central core along which are a number of thin filaments, at the end of which is a single seed in its own little capsule. These seeds are hidden by the sepals of the flower. When the seeds are ripe the filament curls back and jerks the seed up, while the little capsule opens and the seed is thrown out. It is necessary

10 **Exploding capsule of a lupin** Many plants have an exploding device to throw seeds some distance away from the plant to secure for them better chances of germination

to catch the seeds before this happens. The beak turns brown some time before the seeds are actually ripe, so you must look at the capsules that are hidden among the sepals; when they look black, the fruit is ready to be detached. It will probably do its little explosive act in the bag and you may well find the seeds have all been shed, when you come to examine them later. Once the capsule is jerked free of the sepals you have lost the seed. In the geranium family it is only *Geranium* itself that has this explosive mechanism. Erodiums are easily gathered when ripe, while the seed of pelargoniums has a little parachute attached and can be collected as soon as it has unfurled this (it is rather like a dandelion seed), before the seed is blown away. Many plants with pods, like broom and lupins, explode when dead ripe, but since they look like ordinary ripe capsules before this happens there is usually little trouble in gathering them. Some of the Mediterranean spurges, such as *Euphorbia characias*, also have explosive seeds and the capsules only look half-ripe when this happens, so once more it is as well to examine the odd capsule to see if the seeds (which are nearly white) are ready, and if they are, they should be collected at once. Euphorbia seeds need handling with especial care, as they are very different from the majority of seeds. Most seeds are more or less indestructible, unless you take a hammer to them, but the seeds of many euphorbias are very brittle and break up very readily, so it is by no means easy to obtain seeds from outside sources. They are so liable to be damaged in the packet.

Alstroemerias look as though there would be no difficulty in gathering their seed which is held in globular capsules, which turn brown and brittle like most other capsules. However, once the seeds are ready to be dispersed, the capsule explodes and the seeds are thrown away, so you have to be sure to get the capsules in before this happens. There is usually plenty of time, but if it slips your mind for a few days you may find that you have lost all the seed when they come to mind again.

The most explosive capsules are those of the balsams, *Impatiens*. Among these are such popular plants as policeman's helmet (*I. glandulosa*) and Busy Lizzie (*I. wallerana*). Obviously the seeds must complete their ripening after being shed, as it only needs a touch for the capsule to curl back all its segments and expel the seeds. Indeed it is no use picking the capsules in the ordinary way, as they would all explode as soon as you went to touch them. What you have to do is to have your bag in one hand and pick the capsules off by their stalks, so that they fall at once into the bag, where they can explode and eject their seeds in their own time. Here again the capsules have to be gathered while they are still green and the only guide that one has that they are ready to collect is that they are fully grown. There are usually plenty of capsules, which are formed over a long period, so it is possible to open one in order to see that the ovules have started to change colour. Once this has happened and you can recognize the right size capsule, you can start collecting. As we have said the plant has a long flowering season, so that you may find that the first capsules are ready to gather while the plant is still producing flowers. Actually there are not many species of balsam from which it is possible to obtain seeds, since the majority are greenhouse plants and quite bulky, so that the demand is not great.

So far we have been considering seeds which have to be gathered at just the right time, otherwise they may be lost, so you may be happy to turn to the bottlebrushes (*Callistemon* spp.), where you can wait many years before you gather the seed if there is no hurry. These plants are usually either grown against walls or in a cool greenhouse and come from Australia. After they have flowered the stem goes on elongating, while the capsules form a girdle around the stem. They are small, globular and become eventually very hard and woody and they show no sign of opening to release the seeds. Many Australian plants seem to be geared to the bush fires. We have seen how wattle seeds need to be burned to encourage germination and in the same way the capsules of the bottlebrush have to be given some considerable heat to get them to open, although it is also possible to crack them with a small hammer. They are also firmly attached to the branches and have to be taken off with some slight force. Some people put them in a frying pan over a low flame in order to get them to open, but you have, of course, to take care not to overheat them. The moment one pops, you must tip all the other capsules off the frying pan on to some cool surface. After this the capsules should open easily. The seeds are minute, but they usually germinate soon and the young plants grow extremely rapidly and often flower three years after sowing. There are not many plants from which it is so hard to extract the seed, but quite a few antipodean plants seem reluctant to let their seeds go. The manuka of New Zealand (*Leptospermum*) opens its capsules quite normally, but the seeds remain inside for a long time and there need be no mad rush to collect them. They will wait on your convenience, which is a good example that far too few plants follow. However, among these are the rhododendrons and azaleas. The capsules often take a year to ripen and even when they split open the seeds are only released by the wind and it takes a long time before they have all been dispersed, so these too are easy enough to collect.

Once the seed has been collected, it has to be cleaned. This is usually a job for the winter months, when there is not much to do in the garden, but it can be done at any time that is convenient. Seedsmen, of course, have machines for this purpose, but you and I have to do it the hard way. What you need is a table, sheets of paper, a waste-paper basket and seed envelopes, which are easily purchased from any stationers and can, in any case, be replaced by any other envelope. Take a sheet of paper, fold it down the middle, open it out again and spread it on the table. Now take one of your paper bagfuls of seed and tip the contents out on to the paper. You will find a mixture of seeds and capsules. Examine the capsules to make sure that all the seed has been shed and put the empty husks into the waste-paper basket. If any leaves or bits of capsule are mixed up with the seeds, remove these, either by hand or by gentle fanning, which will move the debris, while leaving the seeds intact. Once all the debris has been removed, fold the paper again so that all the seeds fall into the centre fold and shoot them into your envelope. When you have got all the seeds in, seal the envelope, write the name of the seeds on it and store in a coolish place until you wish to sow or to send the seeds away. This cleaning is necessary as it is often the little bits of capsule or dead leaves which bring disease to the young seedlings.

A much more rapid method, but one which requires quite considerable room, is to tip seeds and capsules into a bowl of water. The seeds will sink to the bottom and the debris will float. This can then be removed, and the water with the seeds poured into a funnel, in which a filter paper has been inserted. This will retain the seeds, which must be spread out and dried before being packeted, and you must be quite sure that they are completely dry, which means leaving them around for two or three days. This is labour saving, but the first method is probably safer, as if the seeds were packeted while still even slightly moist they would almost certainly get mildew and be of no use.

UNUSUAL SEEDS

Most seedsmen only stock the more popular plants and it is often very hard to get hold of the seeds of unusual subjects. There are, it is true, a few nurserymen who do offer seeds of plants that the larger firms do not carry, but for a really varied list it is best to join one of the various garden societies which issue a seed list. Among these the foremost are the Royal Horticultural Society, the Hardy Plant Society and the Alpine Garden Society. The R.H.S. gathers all the seeds that ripen in their gardens at Wisley and they also receive seeds from Fellows of the Society. The other societies do not have gardens of their own, but they subscribe to many plant and seed-collecting expeditions; they receive seeds from their members and they may also receive seeds gathered in the wild, both from members travelling abroad and also from those resident in foreign parts. They are thus able to offer an extremely large selection. For example the 1976 seed list of the Alpine Garden Society had no fewer than 3,971 different items, and was by no means confined to alpine plants; there were plants to suit every type of garden and gardener. However, each member is only allowed a certain number of seed packets and this number is often increased if you have sent seeds yourself to swell the list, so it may well be to your advantage to save seeds, even though you or your friends may have no particular use for them. There is almost certain to be someone for whom the seeds of plants that you may consider common will be welcome. Of course you get many other advantages from joining such societies, but the seed list is in itself often worth the annual subscription. Such societies also publish journals and much in the foregoing pages has been taken from writings in the *R.H.S. Journal* (now called *The Garden*) and the *Bulletin* of the Alpine Garden Society.

Other sources for rare seeds are seedsmen in such countries as South Africa, India and Australia who specialize in their native plants. It is not easy to get hold of names and addresses, but, presumably, application to the Agricultural Advisers at

E

Embassies or High Commissions should have some success. Also it is possible to subscribe to foreign botanic gardens and many of these issue a list of such surplus seeds as they may have. These are sold commercially in some cases, while in others it is only necessary to pay a small fee to cover postage and packing. Seeds are allowed into the country free of duty, so that there is no trouble with customs. Still the main source of rare seeds is the work of the amateur grower in raising the plants and later collecting the seed. One might almost say that if you have an uncommon plant it is your duty to see that seeds are collected if at all possible.

8 Hybridization

If we are speaking pedantically a hybrid is the result of crossing different species of a genus. For example the popular hybrid tea rose has the blood of at least four, and possibly six, different rose species.*

The term is used rather loosely nowadays and we hear of F_1 hybrids of cucumbers, when there is no reason to suppose that any other species than *Cucumis sativus* has been involved. These so-called hybrids are the result of crossing two different cultivars and should more properly be termed F_1 crosses. This is all right when we are concerned with single species such as the cucumber or the brussel sprout, but what are we to term the F_1 petunia hybrids? The garden petunia is already a hybrid, so that we can call the plants hybrids accurately enough, but we should not term them F_1. The phrase F_1 designates the first generation of a cross and since the parents of these particular petunias are probably the result of many generations, the term F_1 must be inaccurate here. I am quite unable to think of an appropriate short description of such plants and I only mention the matter here to indicate that botany is by no means so exact a science as many would have us believe. Perhaps we could call such plants 'specially pollinated'.

You may well ask why, with so many natural species, should anyone wish to create hybrids. Well, in the first place there is every reason to believe that many of these natural species originally arose through hybridization. That popular little iris,

* *Rosa gallica* and *R. moschata, chinensis gigantea* and perhaps *phoenicea* and *canina.* The yellow H.Ts also contain *R. foetida* blood.

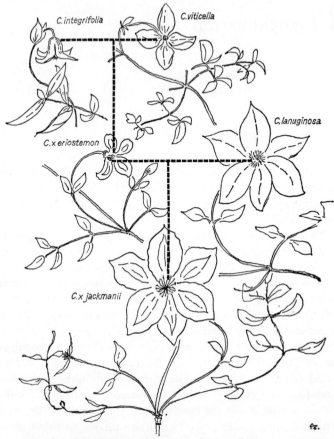

C.integrifolia

C.viticella

C.lanuginosa

C. × eriostemon

C. × jackmanii

fg.

11 **Family tree of Clematis × jackmanii** The parentage is said
to be *C. × eriostemon* crossed with *C. lanuginosa. C. × eriostemon*
was a hybrid between the herbaceous *C. integrifolia*, with entire
ovate leaves and a blue tubular bell-shaped flower, and the
woody climber *C. viticella* with rather small violet flowers and
trifoliate leaves. Both plants are European.

    C. × eriostemon throws up annual climbing stems and has
compound leaves and a flower rather like *C. integrifolia*, but
deeper in colour. *C. lanuginosa*, from China, is only a moderate
climber, is rather tender and has very large white or pale blue
flowers; crossed with *C. × eriostemon*, one seedling produced
the popular *C. × jackmanii*, which is very hardy and has large
deep purple flowers.

I. pumila seems to have arisen through the accidental hybridization of *I. attica* with *I. pseudopumila*. *I. pumila* is found wild
over much of southern and central Europe, while its parents
are both confined nowadays to small portions of Greece and
Sicily. We have all heard of the term 'hybrid vigour' and it is this
extra vigour which tends to make hybrids larger and more
floriferous than either of their parents. *I. pumila* has proved
itself a far more vigorous plant than either of its parents. After
sufficient generations natural selection will 'fix' a wild hybrid,
so that it behaves like any other species, which, indeed it has
become. One of our common weeds, the common hemp nettle,
Galeopsis tetrahit is apparently a natural hybrid between *G.
speciosa* and *G. pubescens*, and there is no reason to suppose that
that is an isolated instance. Where two or more species are in
close proximity, hybridity may well occur if conditions are
right, such as simultaneous flowering and compatibility and
if the resultant hybrid exhibits greater vigour than its parents,
it may end by ousting them. No one knows what the ancestor
of the dahlia looked like.

So one advantage of making hybrids is that one produces
plants with extra vigour, which may well make them more
floriferous and ornamental. Another aim is to introduce the
desirable characteristics of tender plants into other plants that
are hardy. For example, during the 1820s the deep red Himalayan *Rhododendron arboreum* was brought into cultivation and
this was the first large-flowered red rhododendron known.
Unfortunately it was only in Cornwall that the plant could be
grown out of doors with any hope of success and in most
places it had to be grown in a greenhouse. The early breeders
crossed this plant with the hardy large-flowered rhododendrons
then known, RR. *caucasicum*, *ponticum* and *catawbiense*, and
succeeded in producing red-flowered rhododendrons that were
as hardy as their seed parents, although they mainly tended to
have the earlier flowering of the pollen parent. From this modest
beginning came the innumerable rhododendron hybrids that
we have today, which have transformed gardens more than
any other plant.

There are other possible advantages from hybridizing. It may be possible to transform a plant with attractive flowers, but a gawky and ragged habit, into one with equally pleasing flowers, but a more attractive appearance. Also it may be possible to extend the flowering season, as happened with the first rhododendrons. Moreover, second generation hybrids may well extend the colour range of various flowers. Usually, although not invariably, the first generation tends to produce a plant that is intermediate between its parents. Thus if you cross a tall plant with red flowers and a short plant with yellow flowers, you may reasonably expect a medium-sized plant with orange flowers. If these hybrids are crossed amongst themselves and also back-crossed to either of their parents, the resultant plants will be infinitely variable in size and colour. This is assuming that the original first generation is fertile and can set seed, but as this is not always the case it is not always easy for the amateur to get beyond the first cross. Moreover, sometimes there is a hybridity bar between species, which one might think were compatible, so that all attempts at cross-pollination fail.

Most hybridizing is done nowadays by professional growers, although there are many amateurs working with rhododendrons and lilies, but there is no reason why anyone with a garden should not indulge in this for a hobby, as no expensive apparatus is necessary. The basic technique is simplicity itself, consisting simply of putting the pollen of one parent on to the stigma of the other and waiting to see if the flower is pollinated and seeds are set. If so, they are gathered and sown in the usual way. Matters are not, however, quite as simple as this sounds. If you look at a flower, let us say a poppy, you will see inside the petals a great number of thin filaments at the ends of which are little club-like swellings. These are the anthers, which, when ripe, open to discharge pollen. In the centre is a round, ridged body. This is the pistil and the ridges are the stigmas. Most flowers tend to have a much more slender pistil, usually only slightly thicker than the stamens, with a sticky tip. The tip is not sticky all the time and until it becomes so there is no sense in trying to apply pollen, as it will not retain it. Usually nature goes to great pains to prevent flowers pollinating themselves and in any single flower either the pollen ripens before the stigma is ready or the stigma is ready before the pollen ripens. This is one of the reasons why plants bear more than one flower, so that at any one time there are both ripe pollen and receptive pistils, *but not in the same flower*. It may be possible for one flower on a plant to pollinate another flower on the same plant, but it is usually impossible for the pollen of a single flower to get on to the stigma of the same flower. Sometimes nature goes to even greater lengths, by producing plants with different lengths of stamens and pistil. Most of us know that some primroses are what are termed pin-eyed, where only the tip of the stigma is seen in the centre of the flower and some are thrum-eyed and in the centre of the flower is a ring of anthers and no stigma visible. To put it more generally some plants have flowers with long pistils and short stamens, while in others the positions are reversed. Moreover, only pollen from the short stamens will fertilize the long pistils and vice versa. Thus, if you only have pin-eyed primroses, it is extremely unlikely that you will ever be able to get any seed. It is possible to get seed from thrum-eyed plants, but it necessitates hand pollination and even then is not always successful. There are other plants that exhibit the phenomenon of heterostyly, as it is termed, and the would-be hybridist must be aware of such phenomena. (The only genera that occur to me are some forms of *Oxalis* and *Lythrum*, but there are probably many others, although not, I think, in many garden plants.)

Pollen is always easy enough to see; usually it is yellow, although it can be other colours and is easily recognized as a fine dust. Anyone who has smelt a madonna lily and found his nose coated with yellow pollen, will have no doubt of that, but it is not always to easy to see when the stigma is ripe. As we have said, many end in a knob which when ripe exudes a sort of sticky sugar to which the pollen grains will adhere. On the other hand the style of the geranium is delicately branched at the end, when fully grown, and no actual platform for the pollen is detectable without a lens. The style of many irises looks more like a small petal than anything else and here again it is not easy to see when it is ready and you may have to apply a little pollen and see if it adheres or not. Pollen can be kept for months if necessary, provided it is dry and cool, but the stigma is only receptive for a few days at the most, so it is recognizing when this is ready that is the great essential in hybridizing.

Assuming that you have done all that, the most usual procedure is as follows: although it is very unlikely that the stamens of a flower could pollinate it, there may be a short overlap so as soon as the flower that you wish to pollinate is open, remove all the stamens. You can also, if you wish, remove the petals, which are only there to attract the insect pollinators, which you don't want. Even so you want to be sure that no insect gets to the stigma before you do, so the flower can be covered with a paper bag. To get the pollen you can either tip some into an envelope or simply wait until it is ripe (assuming that your two parents are flowering simultaneously). If there is a gap you must collect and bag the pollen. If you put the ripe anthers upside down in the bag and remove them after a day or so, you will have plenty of pollen with which to work. As soon as the stigma is ripe, you put on the pollen. Most people use a very fine camel-hair brush for this purpose, but I do not know that camel-hair is essential and probably any fine brush will serve. Once you see that the pollen is sticking on the stigma, replace whatever covering you have used and tie a label on the plant. On this label you either write down what the cross was or you just put a number and have a special book in which you write down both the number and the actual mechanics of the cross. Thus your entry could read: 257. *Rosa moyesii* x *R. sericea*. The usual convention is to put the seed parent first and the pollen parent second, but the great thing is to be consistent. The use of numbers is preferable, firstly because it is tedious to write too much on a ladel and secondly because it is unlikely that you will only pollinate a single flower; it is obviously safer to write '257' a dozen times than to write out the parentage that often. Other information that is worth noting is the date when the cross is made and, if you are really scientific, the number of good seeds you obtain.

You will now want to watch your plants and once you see the capsules beginning to swell you can remove the covering and wait for them to ripen. Once this is done you collect the seed and sow in the usual way; probably in the spring, but if the parents are ones that require special treatment, whenever that is indicated. Very often the least vigorous looking of the seedlings are the ones that have the most handsome flowers, so it is advisable to 'grow on' every seedling you have until you see the results. Once you do you must be ruthless and destroy any plant that is not an improvement on the parents. Everyone's goose is a swan and it is not easy to decide that the plants over which you have taken so much trouble are no use, but if you do not exhibit an iron will your garden will soon be full of very ordinary plants and you will have no room left for further experiments.

It is very improbable that the amateur will make much, or indeed, any money out of his work. It is not usually by a lucky chance that such plants as the rose 'Peace' are produced and the chance of producing a best seller is as remote as winning the pools. It can happen, but for heaven's sake, do not make that your object in hybridizing. For the amateur the interest in making hybrids is just in creating new plants, which may show either different colours, or larger flowers than their parents or may even flower at a different time of the year.

By and large there is not much point in the amateur working in fields already well covered by the professional breeders. It is very unlikely that you can do anything with, for example, petunias. It is remotely possible that if you got hold of one of the original wild species, native to the Argentine, and crossed this back to the existing hybrids that you might be able to at least introduce a different habit into the resultant plants, but it is not very likely. When the original hybrids were made in the late 1830s, some growers could produce a single plant that was 150 cm (5 ft) across and though such plants are not wanted

commercially, they could well be fun to grow. There are, however, some plants that have not been extensively hybridized
and there might be possibilities there.

It is reasonable to work only with different species of the
same genus, or with species and hybrids of this genus. A few
intergeneric hybrids are known—in orchids there are a lot—
but they are not common and usually one genus will not cross
with another. Hybrids are more likely to be fertile if both
species have the same chromosome number and this can be
ascertained by consulting a book such as Darlington and
Ammal's *Chromosome Atlas of Cultivated Plants*. There is not
space in this brief study to explain why this should be so, but
it is a good working hypothesis, although exceptions can be
found. We have seen that very often it is the second generation
of hybrids that show the greatest variability but this is not
possible if the first generation is sterile and sets no seed. Even
so it may still be possible to use the pollen from these sterile
hybrids on either of the parents, although in that case it is
reasonable to suppose that many of the offspring will appear
indistinguishable from the parent on which it has been back-
crossed. Any unusual colour break should be self-fertilized—
that is to say pollinated by another flower from the same plant
—in the hope of perpetuating this. If the colour has been
caused by the emergence of what is popularly, but inaccurately,
known as a recessive character, it is quite easy to fix this by
self-pollination and the colour will be preserved as long as
self-pollination is persisted in. If it is not so caused the plant
can only be increased by asexual propagation, e.g., by cuttings,
or layers.

In selecting your parents it is worth paying some attention
to the actual physical character of the flower. If one parent has
a long pistil and the other a short one, it is best to put the pollen
from the long-pistilled flower on to the shorter one. Normally
the pollen from the plant with the long style will throw out a
tube to reach the ovules longer than that of the short-styled
plant and if the cross were made the other way the short-styled
pollen might not be able to produce a long enough tube to

reach the ovary, whereas no trouble will be found the other way around.

In theory it should make no difference which is the pollen and which is the seed parent, but in practice the same cross may give different results if made in different ways and the old hybridists, when trying to put the characters of tender plants into ones that were hardy, had no doubt that it was important for the seed parent to be the hardy one. We still do not know much about what is termed extra-nuclear inheritance and it is probably best to stick to the old method in such cases. The old hybridists also noticed that the habit of the plant seemed most affected by the seed parent, while the pollen parent appeared to affect the flowers.

It should, perhaps, be noted that it is not always necessary to indulge either in hybridizing or in scientific pollination to produce new plants. The Reverend William Wilkes bred the Shirley poppy simply by noting an ordinary wild poppy that had a white edge to its petals, sowing the seed derived therefrom and continuing in this way, throwing out all seedlings that reverted to the ordinary corn poppy and keeping all seedlings showing some variation. He persisted in this for several years eventually ending up with the popular strain we know today. In the late eighteenth and early nineteenth centuries the florist's ranunculus was available in many more colours than we know today. In the 1830s at ranunculus shows there were classes for ranunculus in among other colours, light purple and grey, black, buff, olive and coffee colour, besides various picotee and mottled flowers. These had all been raised from the ordinary *R. asiaticus* and though they are lost now, it should be possible by raising seedlings and selecting for these colours to reintroduce these lost shades into the species.

It is for the amateur to decide for himself what plants to try to hybridize, but one might suggest phlox, which has a large number of species all with the same chromosome count and which can produce flowers from April until September and, in the same family, polemonium. I personally obtained, fortuitously, a hybrid between *P. coeruleum* and *P. carneum*, with sapphire-blue flowers, but it has proved almost completely sterile. There are many other species with which one could work. The choice is infinite and it depends so much on the grower's perception of the inherent possibilities in various plants that any suggestions are of little use. By no means everyone would want to grow hybrids, but I hope for those who do this brief essay will prove helpful.

⑨ Some unexpectedly quick results

Although we may usually expect to see the first flowers of most herbaceous subjects in the second season after sowing, we tend to think of long waits in the cases of shrubs and bulbs and often with some justification. There are, however, a number of both woody and bulbous plants which come into flower remarkably rapidly from seed and in this chapter these will be enumerated with any cultural notes that may be necessary. Although many of them will flower in the second year from sowing, it is usually in the third year that you can confidently expect to see the results of your work. When you compare the difference in price between a packet of seeds and a single shrub, you will appreciate that the wait is a small price to pay; the more so as you usually have to wait two years before a purchased shrub is again growing away with energy.

Woody plants

Abutilon. *A. vitifolium* is a native of Chile and makes a tall shrub of a rather spire-like habit. It is more or less evergreen—it sheds some but not all of its leaves in the winter—with leaves that are somewhat like those of a vine (as the epithet *vitifolium* would suggest), and which are covered with silvery hairs, which give them a greyish appearance. The flowers are somewhat like those of a mallow, about 5 cm (2 in) in diameter and produced in clusters of three or four at the end of a stalk which emerges from the upper leaf axils in late May and June. They are usually lavender in colour, but there is a very attractive pure white form.

A clever bee hybridized this plant with the rather tender *A. ochsenii*, with greener leaves and smaller flowers that are deep violet. This hybrid is known as *A.* x *suntense*, or sometimes *A.* 'Jermyns', and grows with the same vigour as *A. vitifolium*, but usually has flowers that are larger than those of *A. ochsenii*, although most show the attractive violet colour in the flowers. It flowers about a fortnight before *A. vitifolium*. Although it is a vigorous grower it tends to get rather leggy and is best pruned back fairly hard as soon as flowering is over. Of course if you wish to collect seed, this will have to be omitted.

Seeds both of the hybrid and the species are best sown in gentle heat in early spring. As soon as they are large enough I like to pot them individually in small pots and then to pot on when necessary ending up in a 12·5 cm (5 in) pot. As soon as the risk of spring frosts has passed, the plants are put outside and hardened off. Once this has been done I like to put them in their final positions in the open ground, as larger plants do not really enjoy being moved; but you can line them out in a nursery bed if it is essential. The stronger seedlings may well produce a few flowers in the second spring and all of them should flower in the third. The plants have a reputation for being delicate, which I find unjustified. They are not, however, usually long-lived and ten years may be considered a good age. One reason for their short life is that they do not produce a very extensive root system. This makes them very susceptible to wind damage, so young plants should be securely staked and placed in parts of the garden where the force of the wind can be modified by some shelter. Another reason for their short life may lie in the immense amount of seed that they produce and if you have time to remove any capsules you do not want for seed, you may well prolong the plant's life.

Buddleia. *B. davidii* (sometimes met with as *B. variabilis*) is the popular butterfly bush with its long spikes of lavender, white or reddish-purple flowers in August and September. It has minute, dust-like, seeds which germinate very freely and soon grow away at a great pace. They are usually pricked out in boxes when large enough and then transferred to the open ground in mid-June, usually lined out about 30 cm (12 in) apart and put in their permanent positions in the autumn. They may well flower the following autumn, but will almost certainly do so the autumn after that. The June flowering *B. alternifolia*, which has willowy leaves and little clusters of lavender, fragrant flowers in the leaf axils grows equally fast, but may take an extra year before it flowers freely. Indeed all buddleias seem to grow very rapidly from seed, although they do not all come so speedily to a flowering rhythm.

Callistemon. Unless you live in Cornwall you can probably only grow bottlebrushes successfully against a south- or west-facing wall, as these Australian shrubs are somewhat tender. Here again you have dust-like seeds, which are barely visible when they first germinate, so that the speed with which they grow subsequently seems surprising. The species usually available are *C. citrinus* and *C. speciosus*, both with bright crimson stamens. It is the stamens that make the flowers attractive; they have no petals, but the dense bottlebrush of stamens is as vivid as any more conventional flower.

Cistus. Sometimes known as rock roses, the cistus are moderate sized shrubs with large flat rose-like flowers, which only remain open for a few hours, but which are produced in large numbers, so that the flowering season is quite long. They are mainly native to Mediterranean regions, although a few come from the Atlantic coast of southern Europe. They are evergreen with rather attractive, tongue-shaped leaves, which in some species turn an attractive glaucous colour in the winter. Unfortunately, few of them will survive severe frost; *C. populifolius* being the hardiest, but they come readily from half-ripe cuttings as well as from seed, so that they are easy enough to keep going. Most seedlings will flower in their second season, but some of the taller species, such as the white, purple-blotched, *C. ladanifer* may keep you waiting a year longer. The plants vary in height from about 30 cm (1 ft) in *C. hirsutus* to over 180 cm (6 ft) in *C. ladanifer* and *C. albidus*. Most species have white flowers, but *C. crispus* has a rich crimson blossom, while *C. albidus* and *C. creticus* have rosy-purple flowers, which

I personally find rather muddy. *C. parviflorus* has, as its name suggests, small flowers, but they are a delightful clear rose-pink. The related genus *Halimium* usually has rather smaller flowers than most cistus, but two species have attractive silver leaves and they all have yellow flowers. They are, if anything, even more tender than the cistus, but very attractive and worth the trouble of taking a few cuttings every year. Also closely related are the dwarf *Helianthemum*, which have the advantage of being hardy, but which are only suitable for the alpine garden or the front of the border, as they are rarely more than 20 cm (8 in) high.

Colutea. Speed of growth is the main recommendation of the bladder sennas, although the small leaves are attractive and children love to pop the inflated pods. The yellow or reddish flowers are produced rather sparingly over a long period and never make any very brilliant display. The seeds are treated in the same way as those of cytisus, which we will now consider.

Cytisus and **Genista**. The brooms are rapid-growing, although generally rather short-lived shrubs, which come very readily from seed. Seed from some of the coloured hybrids will give very varied results, some of which may be improvements on their parents, but most will probably be just the opposite. The only real trouble in raising these attractive shrubs lies in the fact that they rapidly make a tap-root and that this must not be damaged. I find it advantageous to soak the seeds for twenty-four hours before sowing and then to put two or three seeds in a 7·5 cm (3 in) pot and, if they all germinate, reduce to a single plant. It is possible to sow the seeds in a larger pot and then pot the seedlings up separately, but in that case you have to take great care not to damage the roots. They can be hardened off in their 7·5 cm (3 in) pots and then planted out in their final positions, or you can pot them on into 12·5 cm (5 in) pots, so as to have a larger plant to put out. Most seedlings will flower in the second year, if they have made enough growth in the first season and you can rely on all flowering in the third year. The one plant that may keep you waiting is the Mount Etna broom, *Genista aetnensis*, but this has the advantage of being much longer lived than most brooms and of flowering late in the season, at a time when flowering shrubs are something of a rarity. The Spanish broom, *Spartium junceum*, is another late-flowering broom and needs the same treatment as all the other brooms.

Coronilla. *C. emerus* and *C. emeroides*, the scorpion sennas, are rather dwarf deciduous shrubs with ferny leaves and heads of yellow pea flowers. They are usually hardy, but can be damaged in severe winters; more attractive is the evergreen *C. glauca*, but it is rather tender and needs wall protection in most districts and in any case must be regarded as doubtful north of the Trent. As its name implies the leaves are an attractive blue-green and it seems to flower over a very long period; its main display is in the summer, but after a good summer it will start to flower again in late autumn and may continue. The seeds are treated much as though they were broom seeds.

Euphorbia. There are two forms of the shrubby *E. characias*. The subspecies *characias* has a chocolate blotch inside a green cup, while the subspecies *wulfenii* has slightly larger cups of a rather strange yellowish-green colour and no blotch. They flower very early in the year—in a mild winter they will be in flower in February—and the buds can be damaged by late frosts and in exceptionally severe winters the growths also, but the plant always seems to survive. The seeds are best started in gentle heat and potted up individually as soon as possible as all the spurges seem very resentful of root disturbance. They vary in height from 45 cm (18 in) to 120 cm (48 in) and thrive best in rather poor soil in full sun. Being Mediterranean plants, drought holds no terrors.

Sambucus. The elders grow very rapidly from seed and usually flower in their third season. If you live in the north *S. racemosus* is one of the most handsome of berrying shrubs, but the other elders tend to be rather graceless, unless you have a form with golden leaves and these will not come true from seed. The only other ordinary elder of much distinction is *S. canadensis* 'Maxima', which has a huge panicle of creamy flowers on purple pedicels in late July and August and is very showy at that season. Unfortunately, there is no guarantee that it will come true from seed.

Of course, if you do not mind waiting five or six years to see your first flowers the list is very large. It would include such genera as *Berberis*, *Cotoneaster*, some *Crataegus*, *Davidia* (This makes a tree. It has been known to flower in seven years from sowing, which sounds improbable, but is well attested.), *Deutzia*, *Fuchsia*, *Indigofera*, *Laburnum*, *Lespedeza*, *Leptospermum*, *Magnolia sinensis* and *M. wilsonii* and some of the x *soulangiana* seedlings, *Mahonia*, *Philadelphus*, *Phlomis*, some *Prunus*, most notably the peaches and almonds; the cherries are much slower. *Ribes*, almost all species of *Rosa*, and many *Rhododendron* species flower in their fifth or sixth year, while others will take considerably longer. It is best to consult a specialist on these plants to find the most rapid flowerers, although R. *decorum* is well-known for this feature. *Sorbaria*, *Spiraea*, *Staphylea*, *Syringa*, *Viburnum* and *Weigela* also are generally of flowering size after five years. If you want a tree rapidly, the few hardy *Eucalyptus* species grow at enormous speed. Like so many Australian plants, the seeds are very minute and it is not easy to avoid sowing too thickly. The seeds are sown in February at a temperature of around 15° C (60° F) and the seedlings potted up individually, as soon as they have acquired two pairs of true leaves. Once they have got over this move and are starting to grow away again they may be transferred to a cold frame, if one is available, and in any case moved to a less warm situation. The ideal pots are long and thin and it has been suggested that tubes of black polythene are more suitable, as the young eucalyptus tend to make more root than shoot growth in the early stages. Any roots that emerge from the bottom of the pot should be cut off every fortnight. Once the risk of frost has gone and roots are seen to emerge from the base of the pots, the plants are best put into their permanent positions. The young trees grow very rapidly—they may well be 120 cm (4 ft) tall by their first autumn and require to be securely staked for the first four or five years of their existence. *E. gunnii* is the species most frequently offered. *E. niphophila*, with attractive silvery wood, is exceptional in tending to grow rather slowly at first, although it makes up for it later. They attain tree-like proportions in a very few years.

Bulbs and other monocotyledons

Although the most popular bulbous subjects, daffodils, hyacinths and tulips take many years to attain flowering size, there are a surprising number which develop much more rapidly. It is true that a large number of these require to be treated like gladioli and lifted to be stored free from frost in the winter, but since everyone does this happily with dahlias and gladioli, it is not really particularly irksome. We have already discussed the best treatment for bulbous plants and this applies to practically all those mentioned here. I should perhaps mention that some growers claim that they get more rapid germination for bulb seeds by soaking them for twenty-four hours in cold water before sowing. I have no experience of this myself, but it can certainly do no harm.

Allium. The garlics vary in the time they take to attain flowering size from seed and the time taken seems to correspond fairly closely to the ultimate size of the bulb. Thus those with small bulbs, such as *AA. coeruleum, flavum, moly, ostrowskianum* and *pulchellum* will usually flower the second year from sowing, while other species will take a year or two more. Seed is best sown in the autumn.

Alstromeria. One of the greatest surprises of the Andean expedition of Messrs. Beckett, Cheese and Watson was the great rapidity with which the various Peruvian lilies came into flower. Some, if sown early enough, flowered the same year as they were sown and practically all flowered the second year. Since the seeds germinate somewhat irregularly, it is perhaps best to treat them as though they were herbaceous plants, potting up the young seedlings as soon as they are large enough to handle, which usually means when they have produced three leaves. The plants like to get their roots down as deep as possible, so you want to continually pot on; most plants will flower in a 15 cm (6 in) pot. The popular Ligtu hybrids are slightly slower and may keep you waiting an extra season. They are quite hardy, but we do not yet know about the new Andean species. Seed is usually sown in the spring.

Anemone. *A. coronaria* and *A. pavonina*, the poppy and St. Bavo anemones are treated just like herbaceous plants, with the seed sown in the spring and pricked out like any other herbaceous plant. Most will flower in the second season. The dwarf *AA. apennina, blanda, nemorosa* and *ranunculoides* shed their seeds while still green and it is usually recommended that they should be sown when fresh, although they will not germinate until the following spring. In many gardens they sow themselves around without the grower having to take any trouble.

Anomatheca. The bulb known as *Anomatheca cruenta* should properly be known as *Lapeirousia laxa*, but is better known under its incorrect name. It is a charming dwarf like a wee scarlet gladiolus and flowers very rapidly from seed. It likes full sun and a very well-drained soil and flowers throughout much of the late summer. Seed is sown in spring.

Aristea. See Orthrosanthus.

Babiana. South African bulbs with pleated leaves and spikes of purple, yellow and other colours, some with attractive perfume. Since they start growing in the autumn, they require cool greenhouse treatment; they will probably tolerate a degree or so of frost, but not more. Seed is sown in spring and the plants grow very rapidly, although it may not be until the third spring that they flower well.

Chionodoxa and **Scilla.** The seeds require to be sown in the autumn, and usually take three years to arrive at flowering size.

Crocus. Most species take three or four years to reach flowering size, but *C. tommasinianus* will have some flowers in the second season. In some gardens it seeds itself around so freely as to become tiresome to tidy gardeners, but most people are only too glad to have masses of its lavender or darker purple flowers in very early spring. All crocus seed should be sown in the autumn.

Cyclamen. Most cyclamen species will flower in the third season from sowing, although some seedlings will require an extra year. Since the corms are so expensive, it is well worth showing sufficient patience. It does not much seem to matter when the seeds are sown.

Cypella. This is alphabetically the first of a number of closely allied South American plants, of which tigridia is the best known. They all have quite large bulbs, but come very rapidly from seed, usually flowering in the second season, although some may make you wait a year longer. They flower in summer and have extremely attractive large orchid-like flowers, which only last twenty-four hours, but which are produced in large numbers. They require to be treated like gladioli; the bulbs being lifted in the autumn, dried off and stored away from frost and replanted about May. *C. herbertii* has yellow flowers, *C. plumbea* has large slate-blue flowers, an unusual colour in this group. Sow in spring.

Freesia. We have already described (see page 63) how this is grown so as to get flowers within six or seven months of sowing. They do, however, need to be protected from frost, so a cool greenhouse is essential. Too much heat in winter inhibits flowering.

Galanthus. Snowdrops usually flower in the third year from sowing. The seeds should be sown in the autumn and this would seem to apply even to the autumn-flowering *G. corcyrensis* and its ally *G. reginae-olgae*.

Geissorhiza. At least one nurseryman offers seed of this attractive South African bulb, which is rather dwarf, but with surprisingly large flowers. The treatment is much the same as for babiana. *G. rochensis*, known as wine cups, which has purple-blue flowers with a bright red eye. Seedlings flower either in the second or third season.

Gladiolus. Many of the species of gladiolus flower the third season after sowing. They contain a number of very attractive plants ranging from the flower arranger's delight *G. tristis* with greeny-yellow flowers that give off great fragrance at night to other charmers with colours of almost every size and hue. The spring-flowering types will usually survive if given wall protection, but do equally well in a cold greenhouse. Those that flower after June can be treated like the commercial gladioli; by lifting each autumn, storing in a dry and frost-free situation and planting out in April. *G. byzantinus* (as well as *G. segetum* and *G. illyricus*) are perfectly hardy and can grow outside without any protection. Most species come from South Africa and there are an enormous number of these, all worth growing, and the only trouble is obtaining the seeds. They are easy enough to grow.

Herbertia. Much like cypella, but with rather smaller leaves and flowers. *Herbertia pulchella* has attractive lavender flowers in June.

Hesperantha. South African dwarf bulbs with both spring and autumn flowering species. That most often seen is *H. baurii* (or *mossii*) with bright pink flowers in early autumn. It is hardy in a protected position. The spring-flowering *H. radiata* with white flowers with red-brown stripes outside and *H. stanfordiae* (syn. *H. vaginata*) with yellow flowers needs either the protection of a frame or a cool greenhouse. Seeds flower in two years and should be sown in spring.

Iris. This is probably getting in here on false pretences as all the bulbous iris are very slow from seed. However, there are other species which are more rapid. The Californian irises, *II. douglasii, innominata, tenax* and their hybrids flower the second year from sowing. They form tufts on a short rhizome, come readily from seed but are very resentful of root disturbance so that the seedlings should be potted up individually as soon as they are large enough to handle and put as soon as possible in their permanent positions. *I. kaempferi* and members of the Sibirica group usually flower in the third season, while the popular bearded iris take four or five years.

Ixia. These attractive South African bulbs flower in the third year from spring-sown seed. They can be treated either as cool greenhouse subjects or kept dried off and planted out in

March and then lifted and stored at the end of the season. The same applies to *Sparaxis*, which may take an extra year.

Kniphofia. The red hot poker makes such large plants one would expect them to take a long time from seed, yet most will flower in the second year and all will flower in the third. Seed sown in spring usually germinates fairly fast, but occasionally it takes an unconscionable time to do so and this may upset your arrangements. Evidently fresh seed is the best if it can be obtained.

Lilium. As we have already said *L. regale* and *L. pumilum* flower in two or three years from seed, while the tender *L. formosanum* and *L. philippinense* may flower even sooner. Other lilies vary from three to seven years, but seedlings are liable not to have the virus, which destroys so many purchased bulbs, so the wait is worth it.

Orthrosanthus. A tufted member of the iris family producing branched spikes of rather small, bright blue flowers during the summer. The individual flowers are very short-lived, but there are very many of them and they flower over quite a long period. *O. chimboracensis* may well be hardy in a sheltered situation; it has tolerated quite severe frost with me. The Australian *O. multiflorus* with gentian-blue flowers is probably more tender. Spring-sown seed flowers in the second year. The South African aristea is similar in appearance, but must pass the winter under glass.

Romulea. These relatives of the Crocus come very rapidly from seed and most species can be expected to flower in the second season. The European species *RR. bulbocodium, clusiana* and *linaresii* should have the seeds sown in the autumn. The more showy South African species, which require cool greenhouse treatment are sown in the spring.

Sisyrinchium. All the tufted members of the iris family seem to grow very rapidly from seed and the blue-eyed grass and its relatives will usually flower in the second year. The seed is sown in spring and generally presents no trouble.

Tigridia. The best-known genus in the group which started with cypella and which needs similar treatment. The best-known species is *Tigridia pavonia*, which has been known to flower the same year as it was sown and all the species seem to flower in the second year. Other species are sometimes available and they all sound attractive. Other genera allied to tigridia which are worth looking out for, but are very rarely offered are *Cipura, Calydorea, Mastigostyla* and *Rigidella*. This last sounds particularly attractive with a spike of scarlet flowers.

If you look at a bulb catalogue you will, I think, agree with me that patience is not only a virtue, but very advantageous economically.

Index

Index